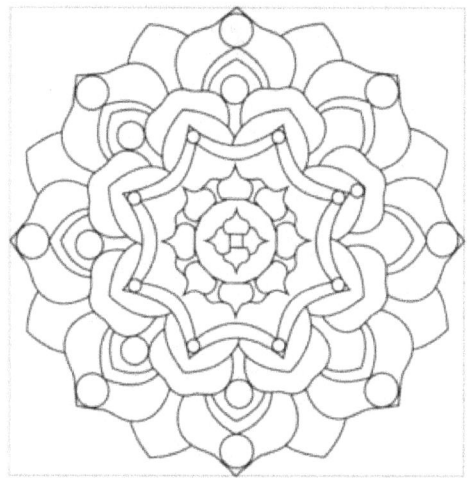

Color Me And Stay Healthy

Coloring Book For Adults

Frank Poku

Get ready to color your way to good health.

Grab some crayons and color pencils and let's go!

Use your imagination and creative senses and begin to

color the artistic patterns in the pages of this book.

The patterns are simple and easy to color.

Just let your imagination loose and the creative talent hidden inside of you

will begin to show itself in the images you will be creating.

The exercise is soothing and pleasurable and as you keep on

coloring, you will begin to feel your stress level come down.

Less stress means good health.

 It's yours, grab It!

DEDICATION

To my good friends, Steve and Doris Leslie, Lawrenceburg, Kentucky.

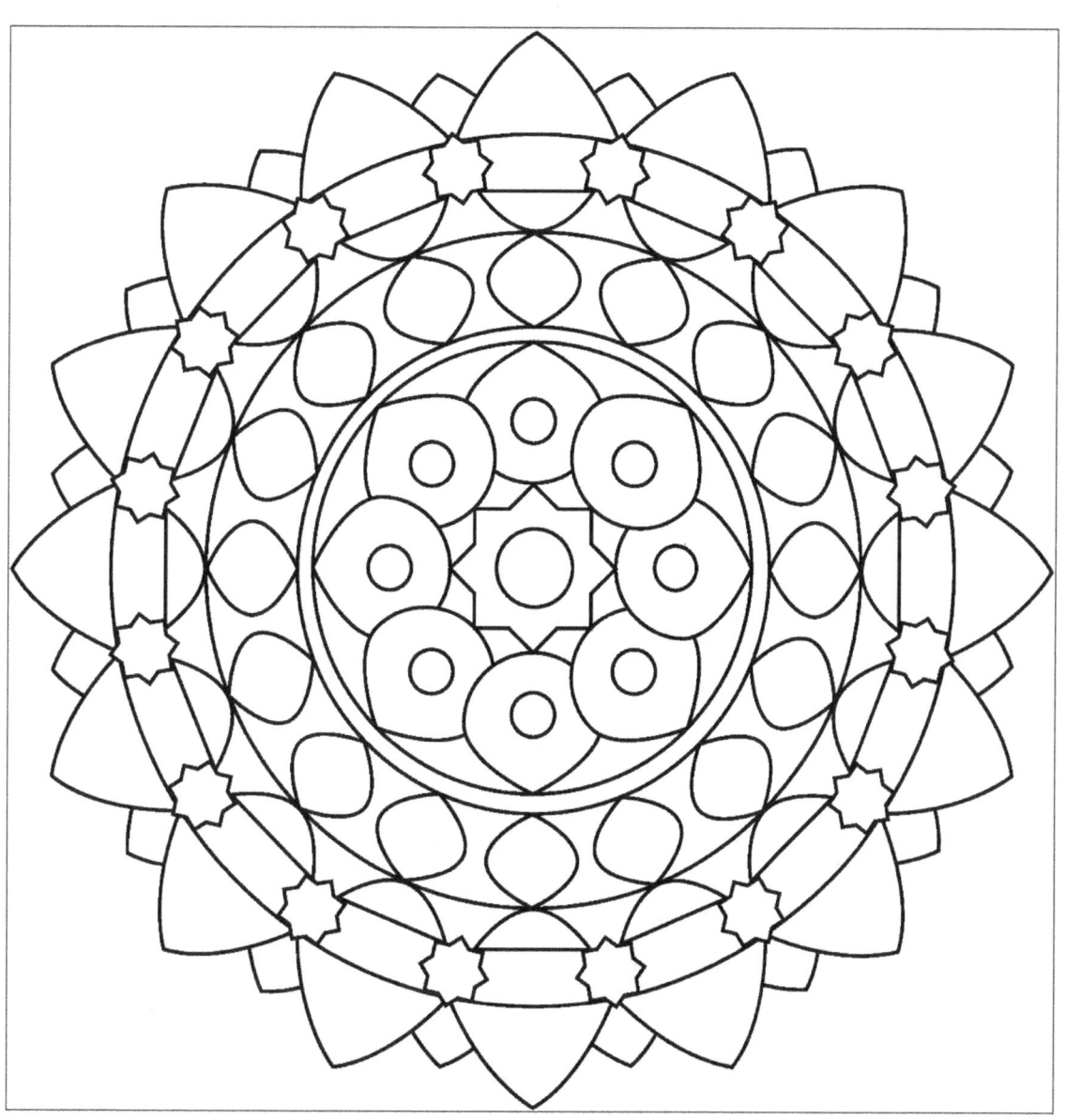

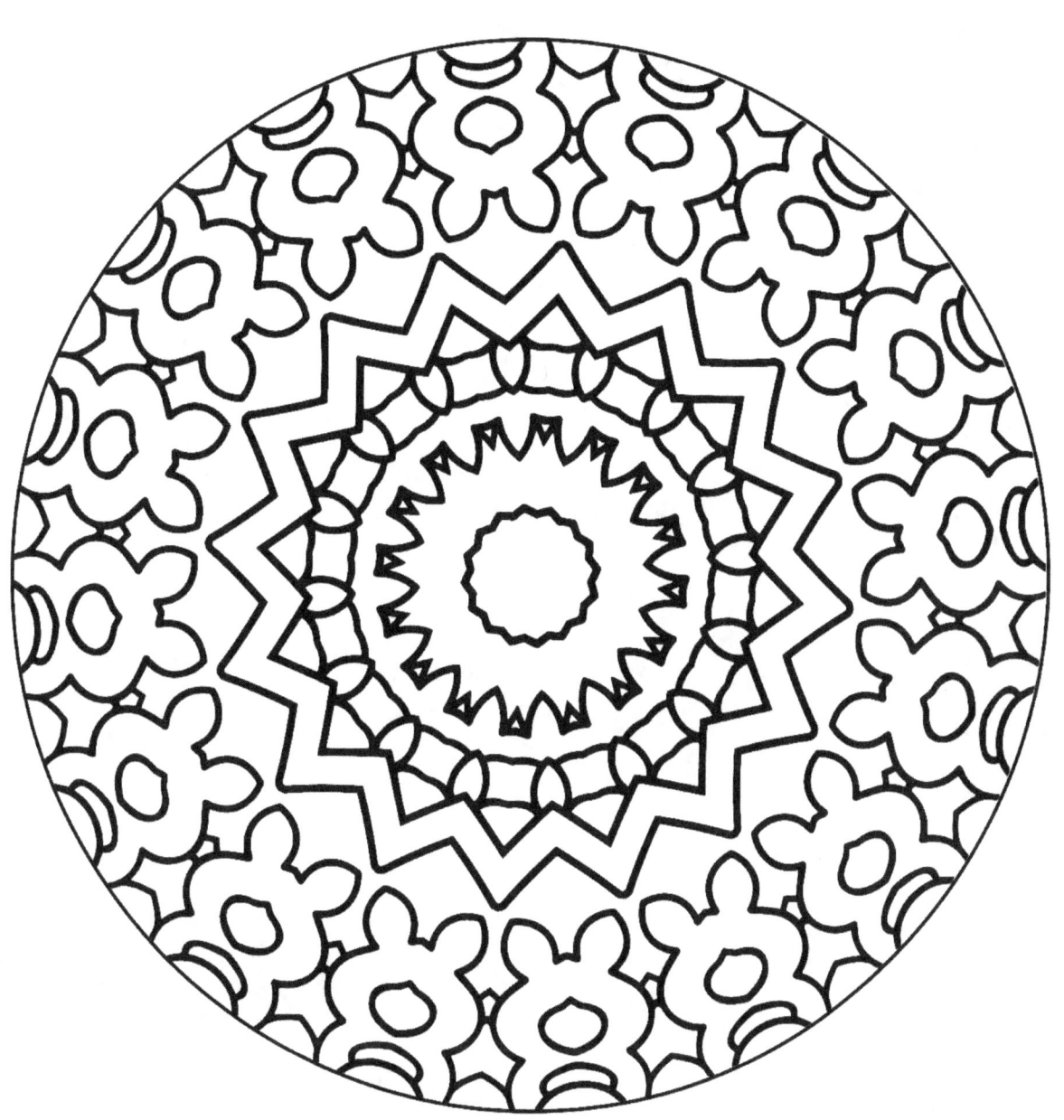

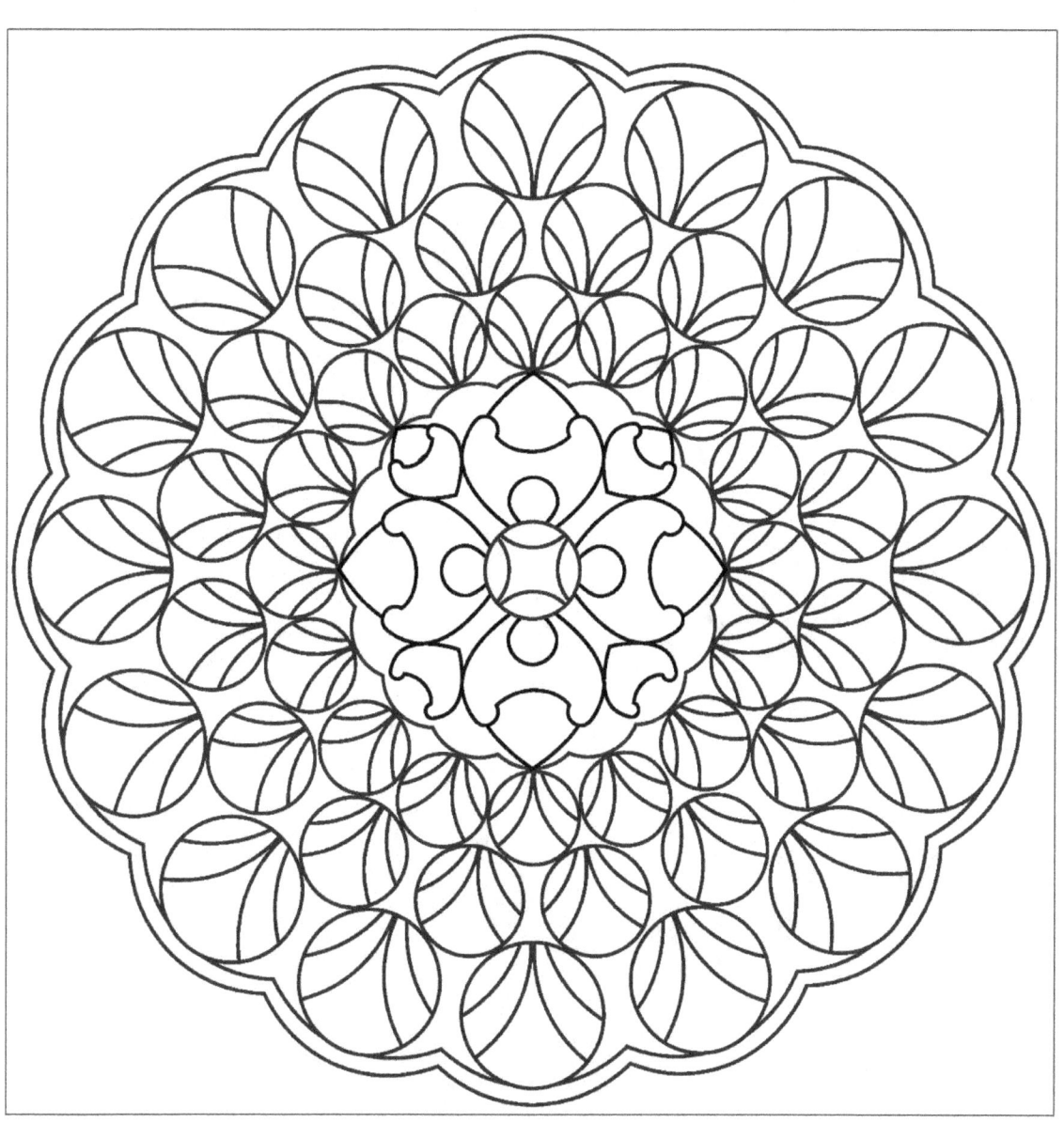

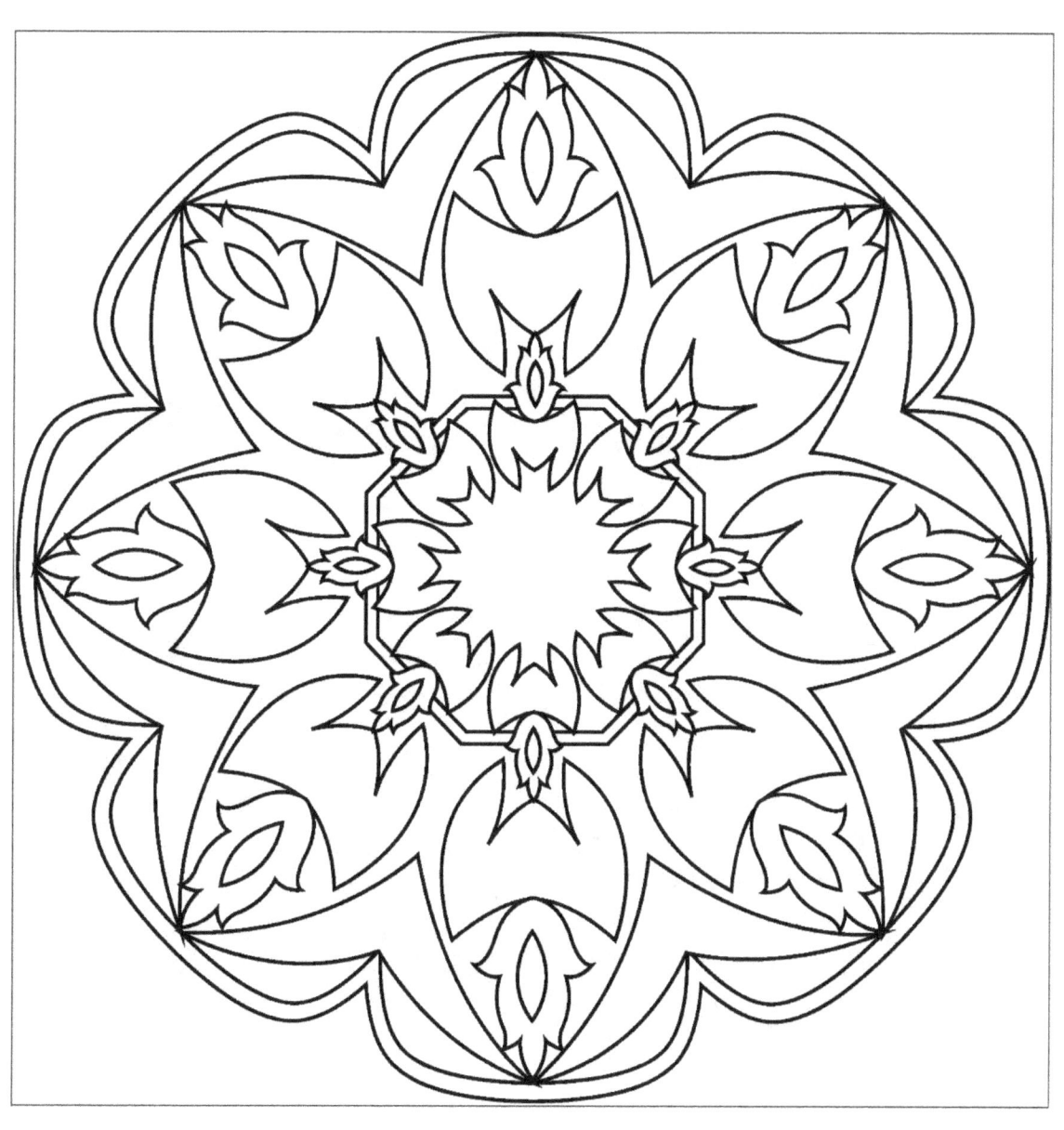

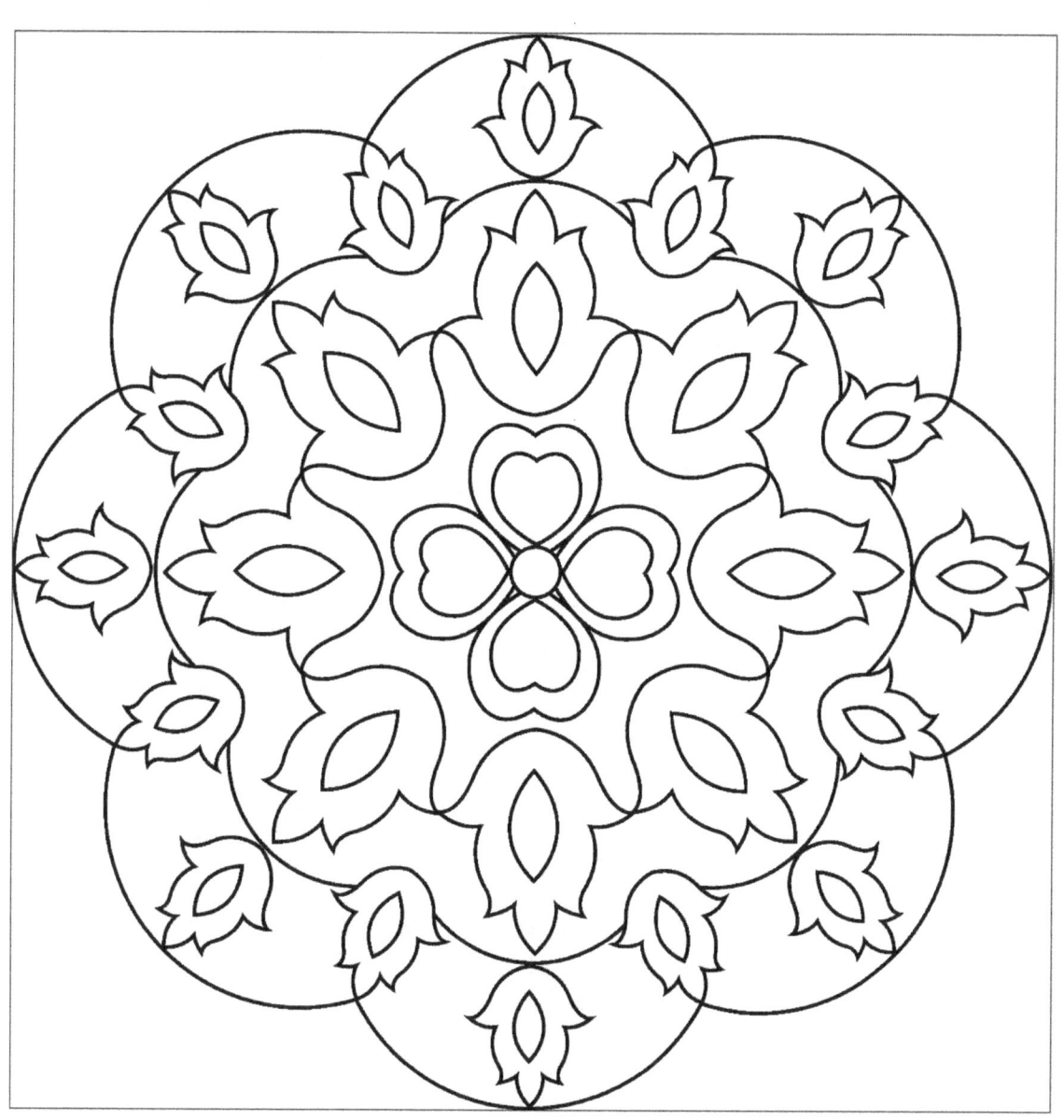

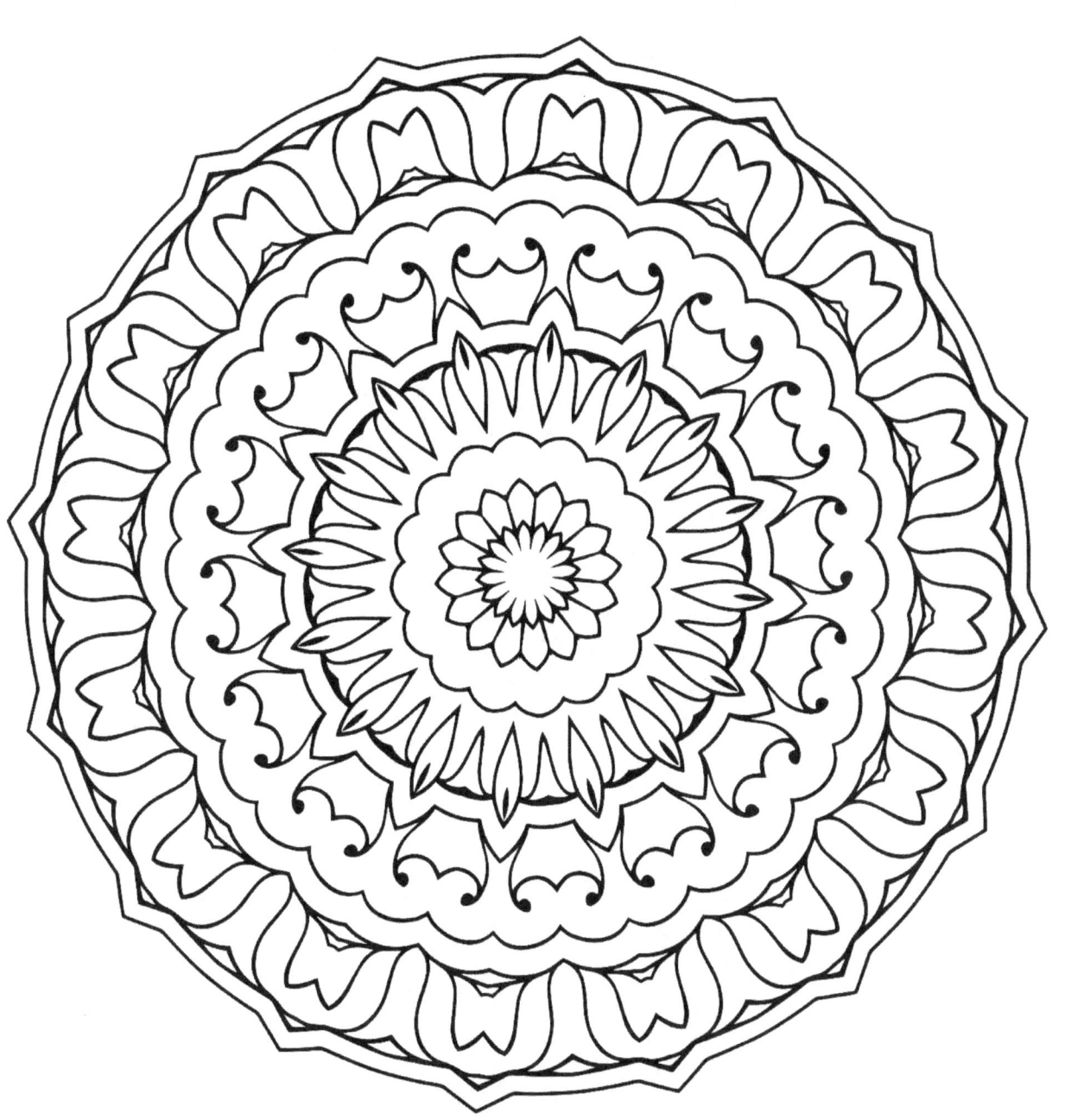

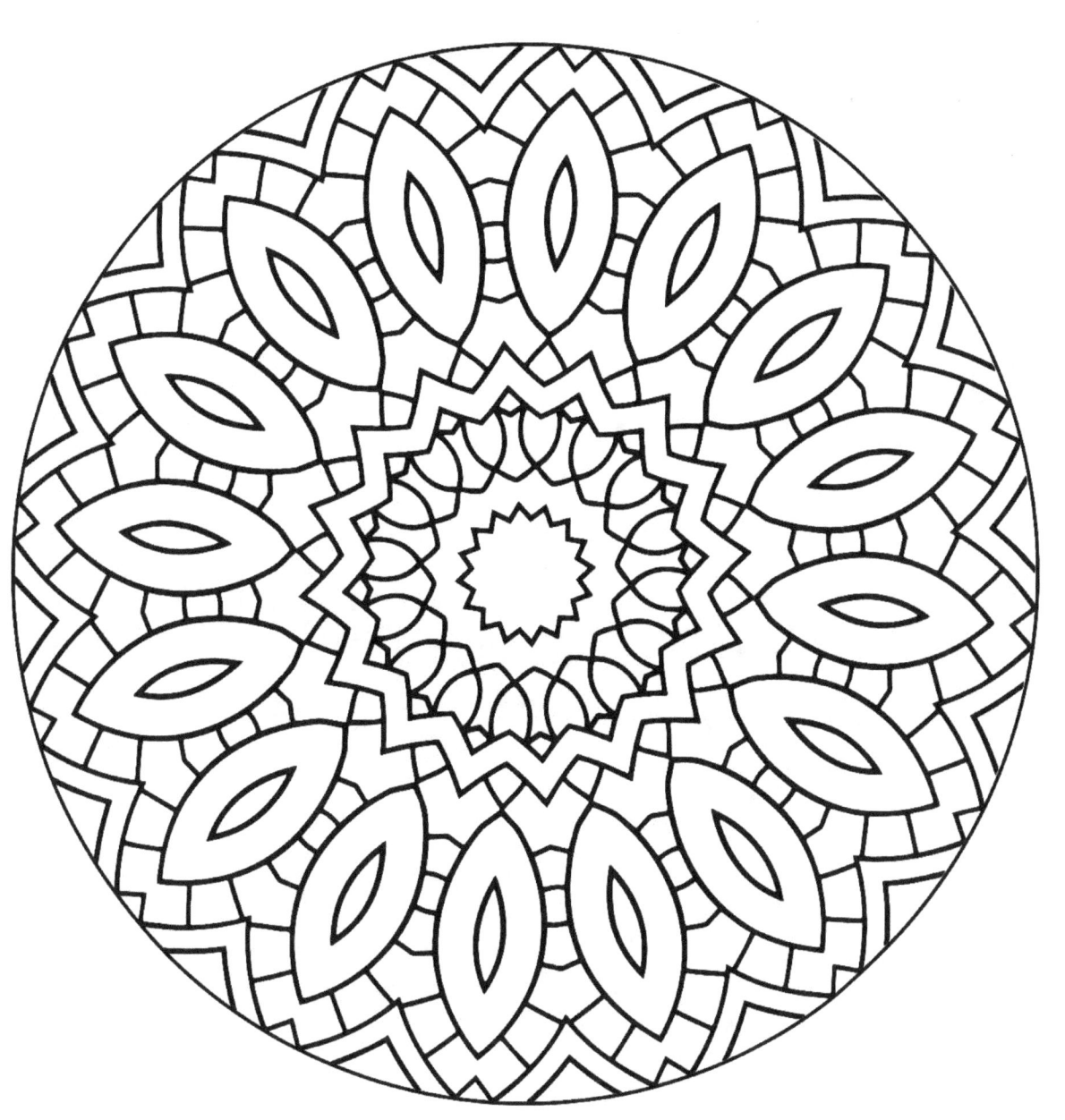

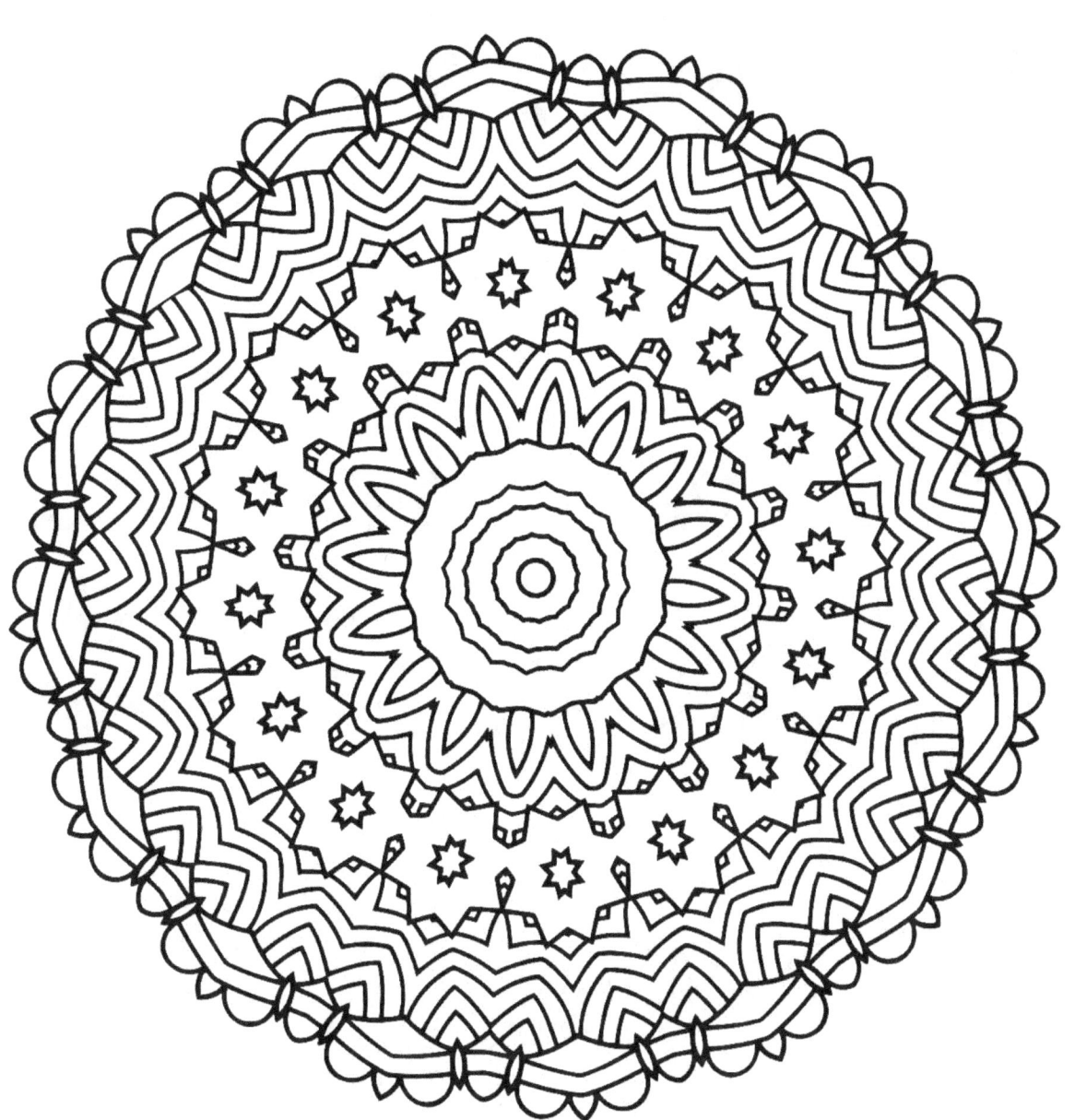

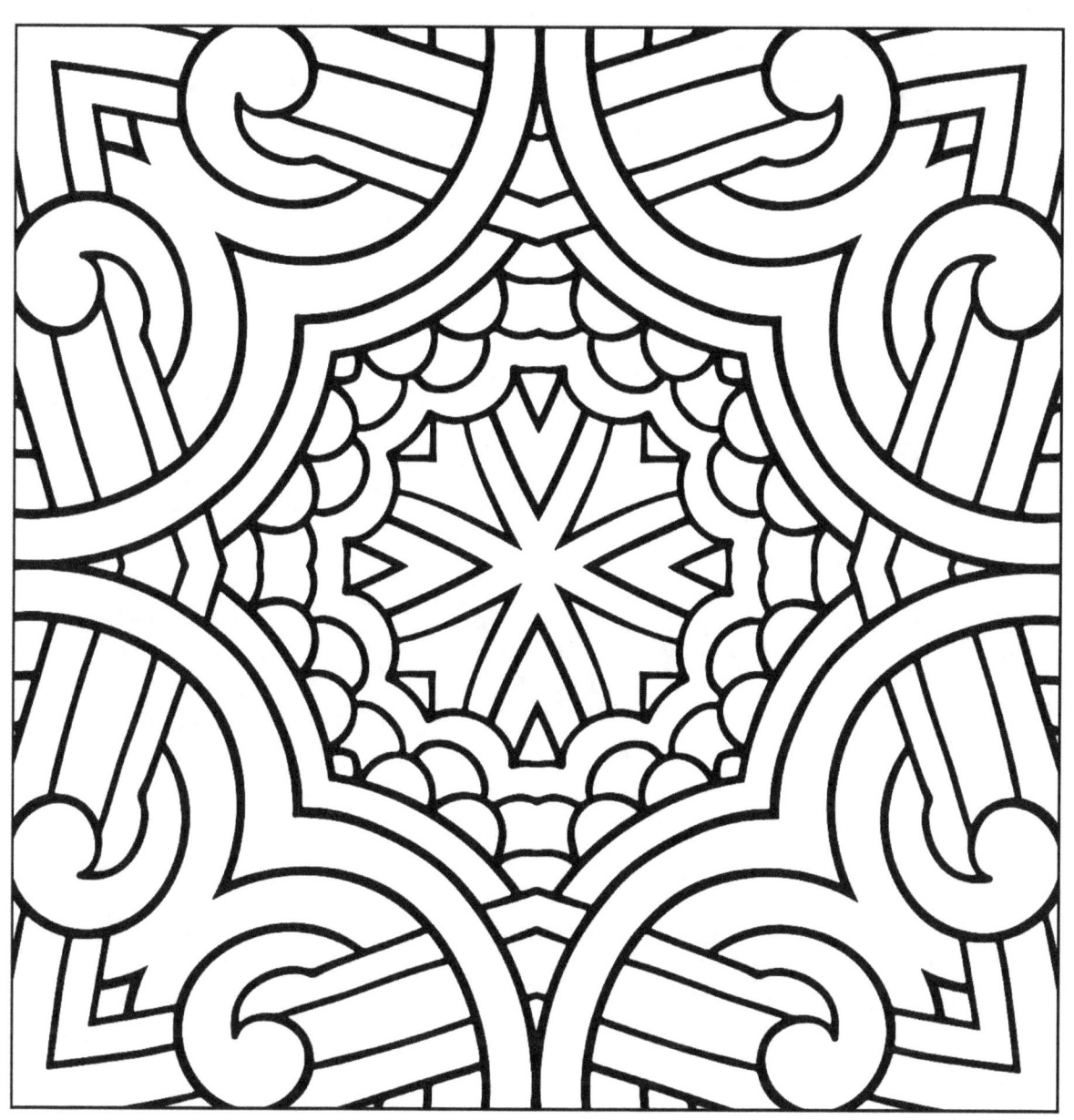

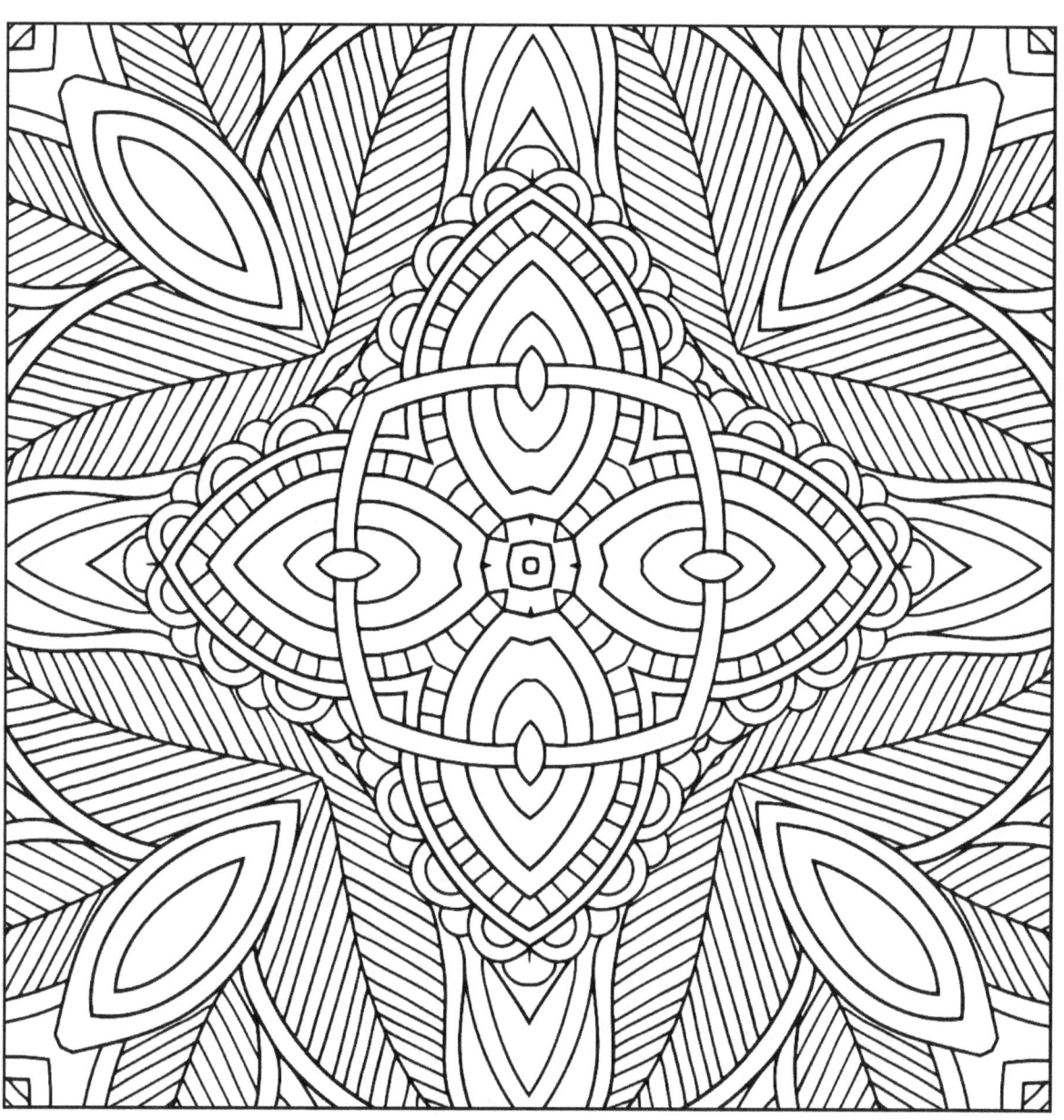

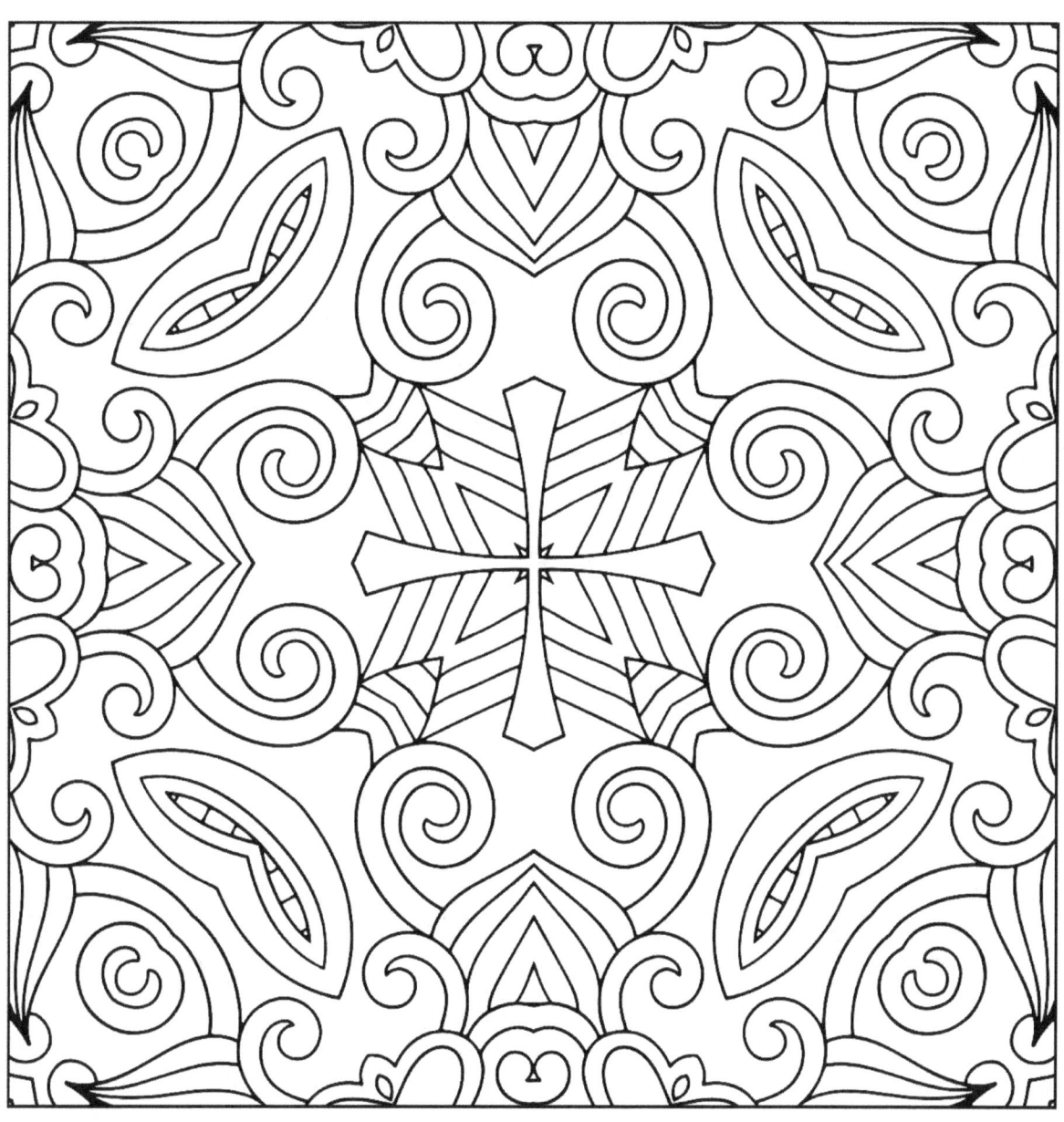

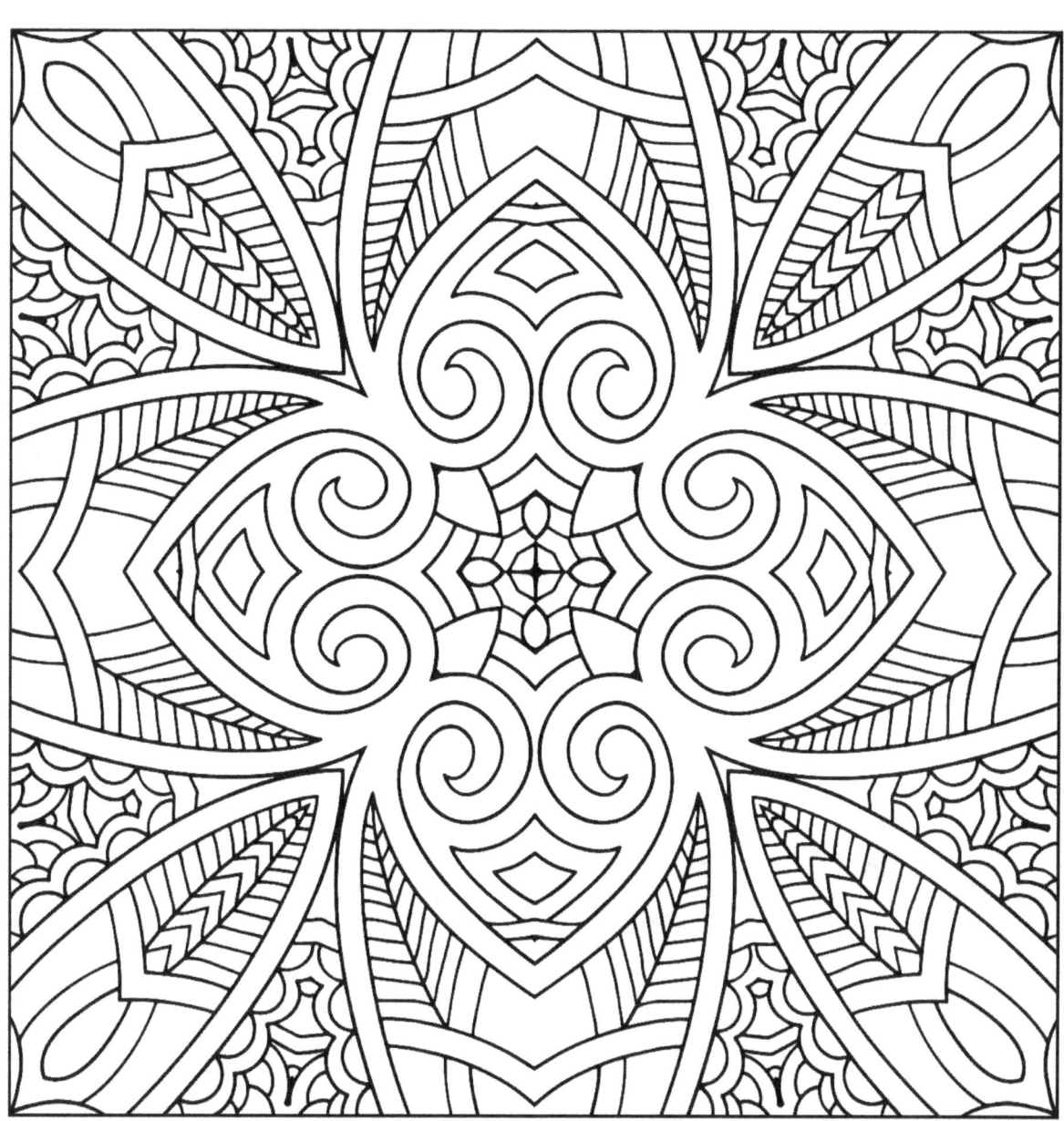

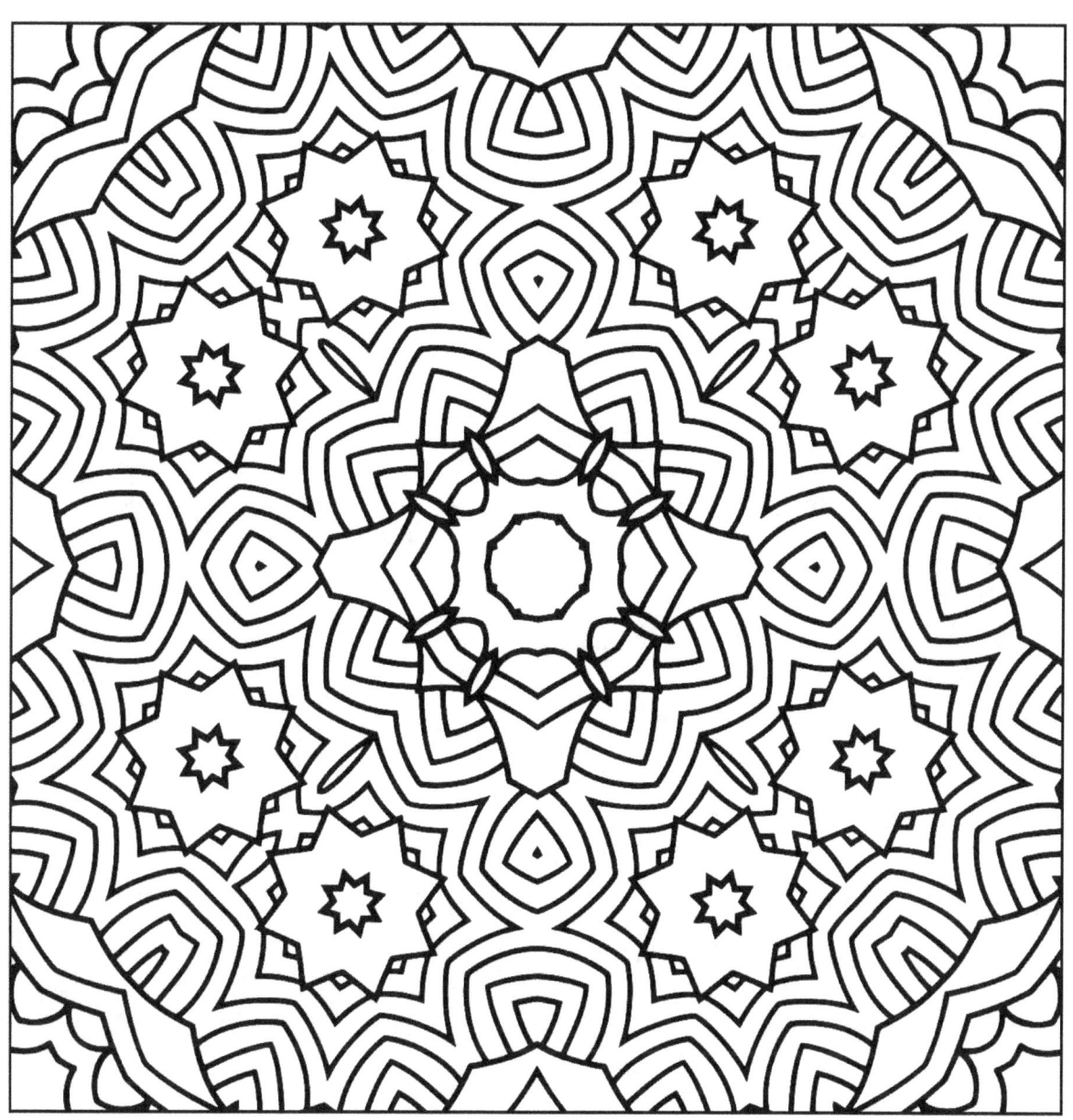

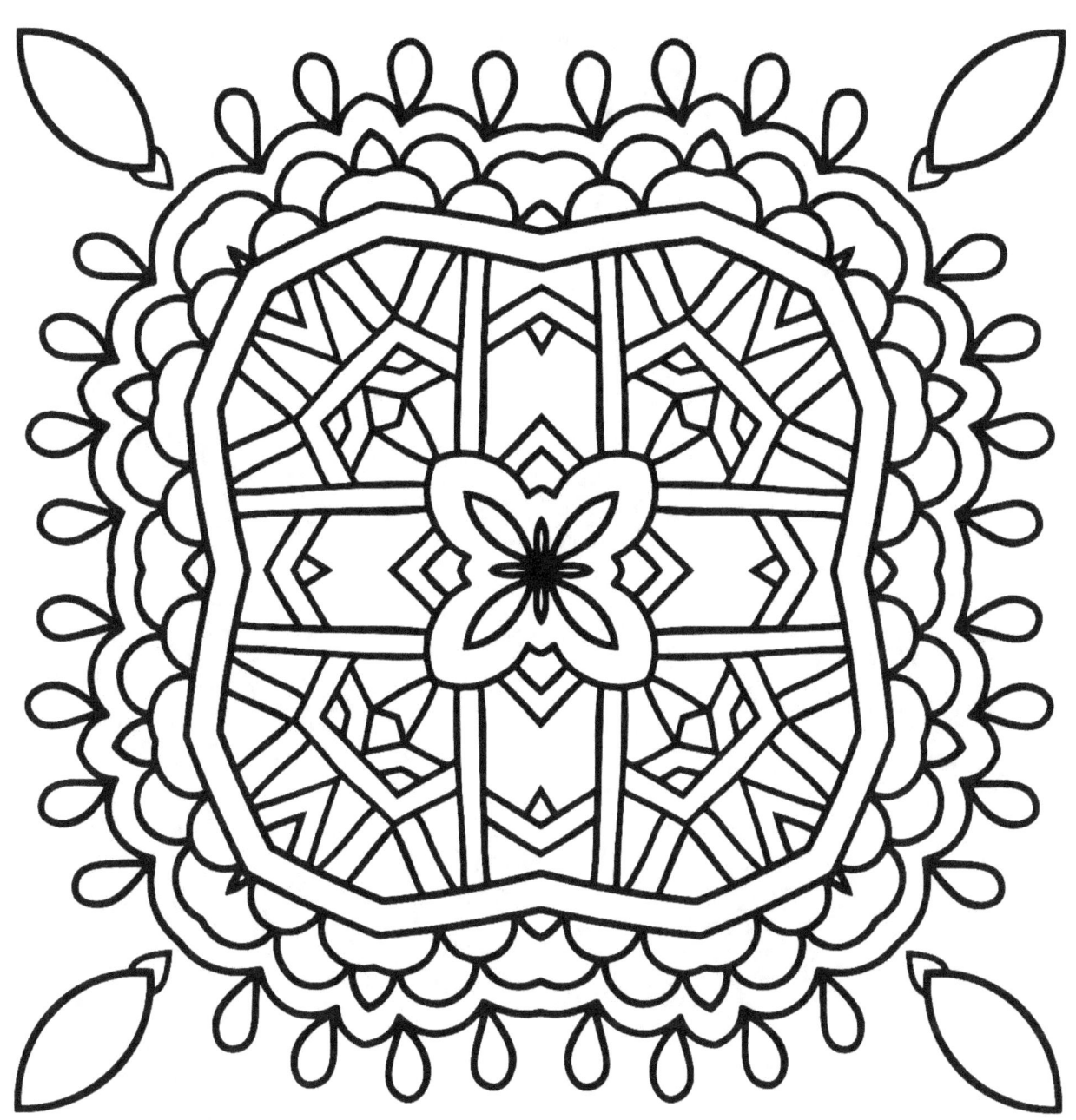

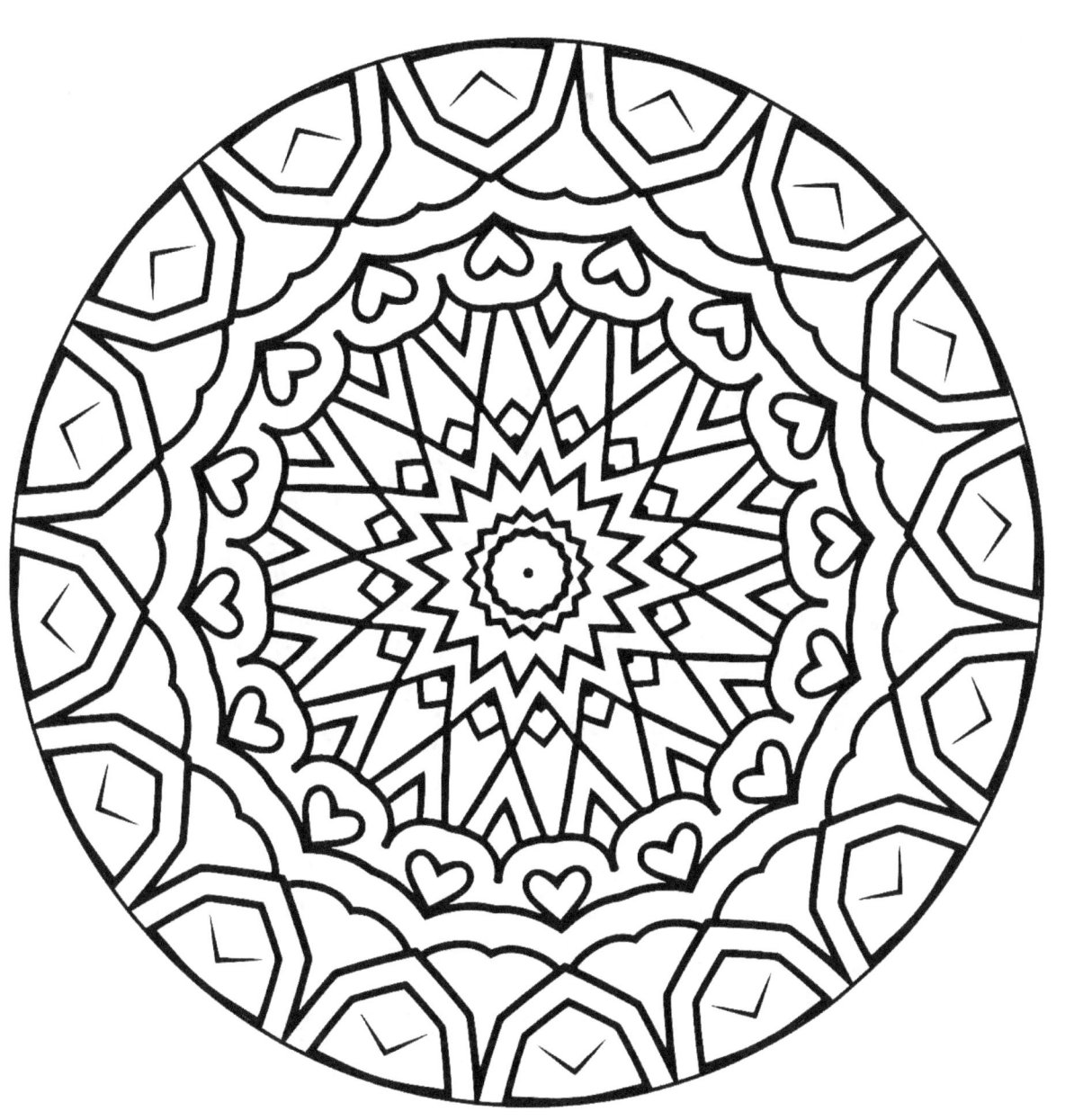

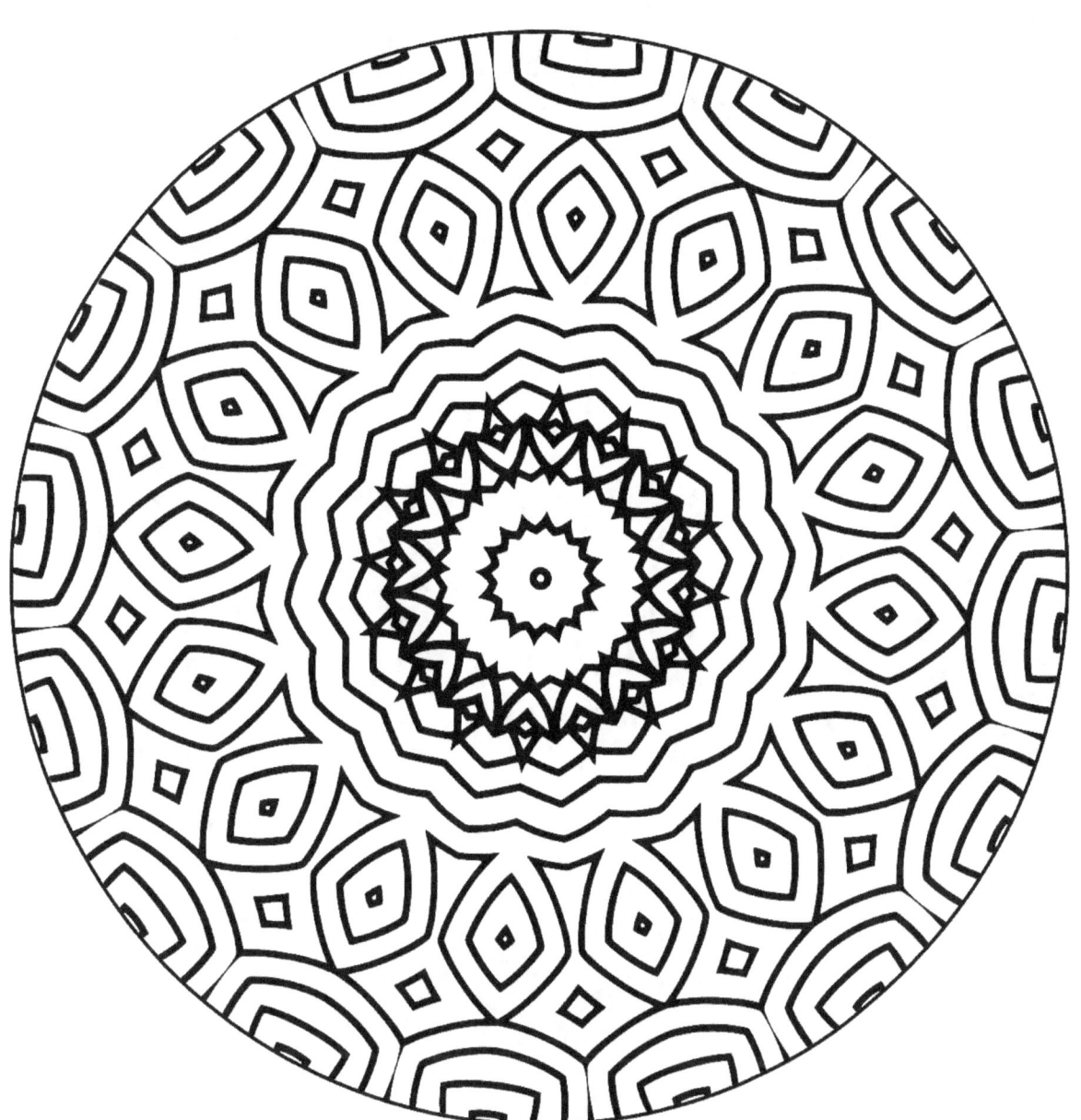

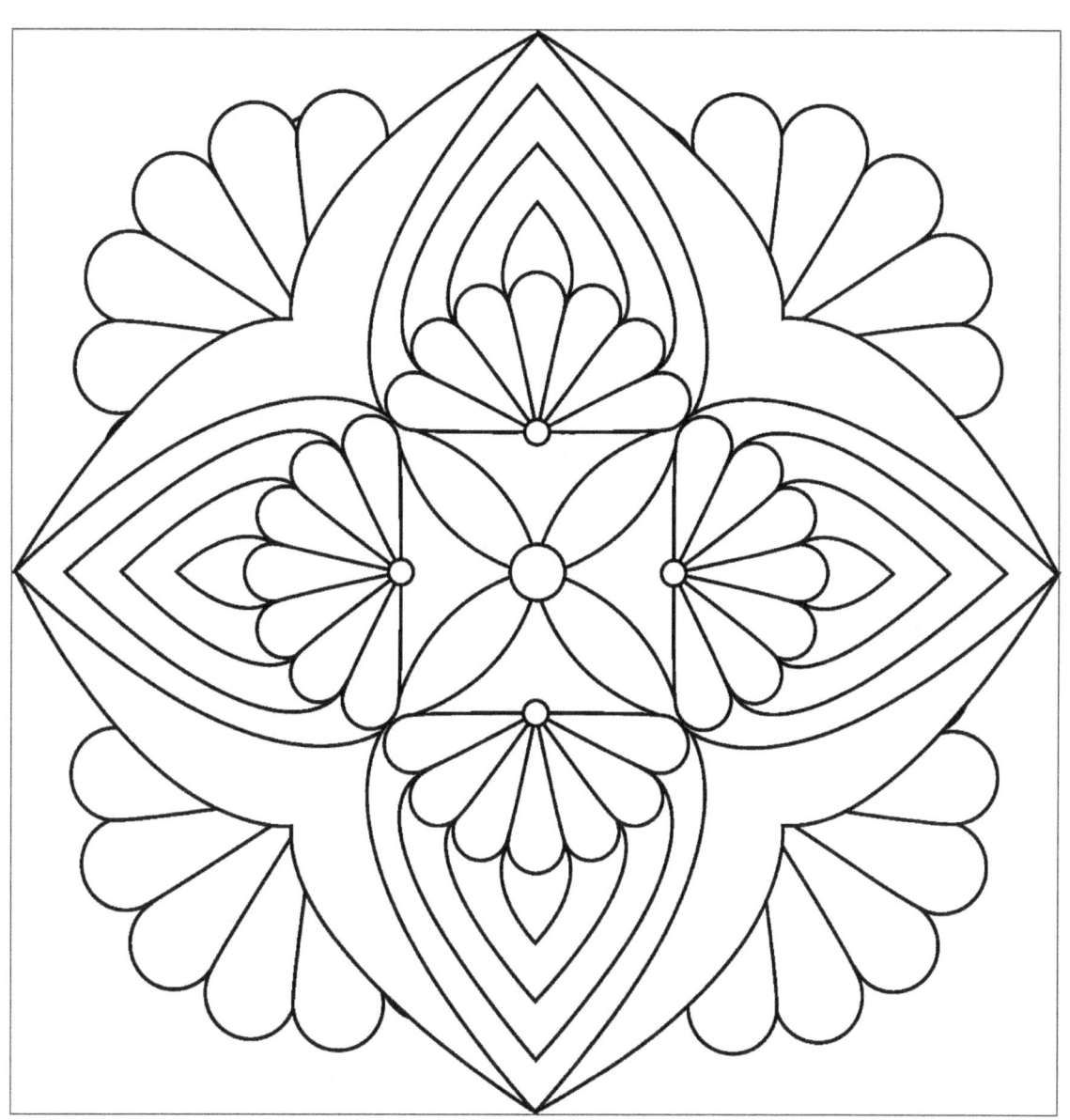

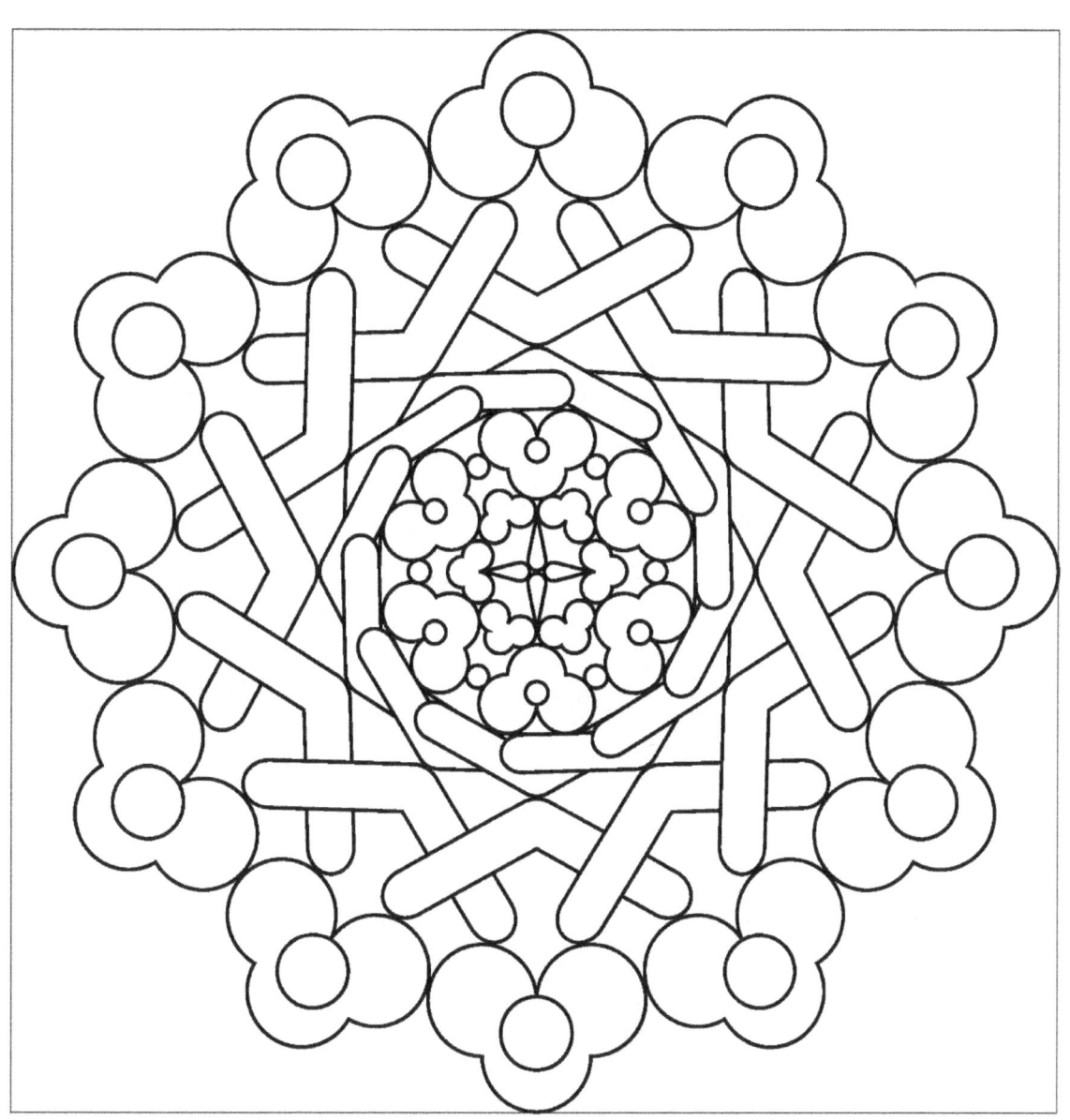

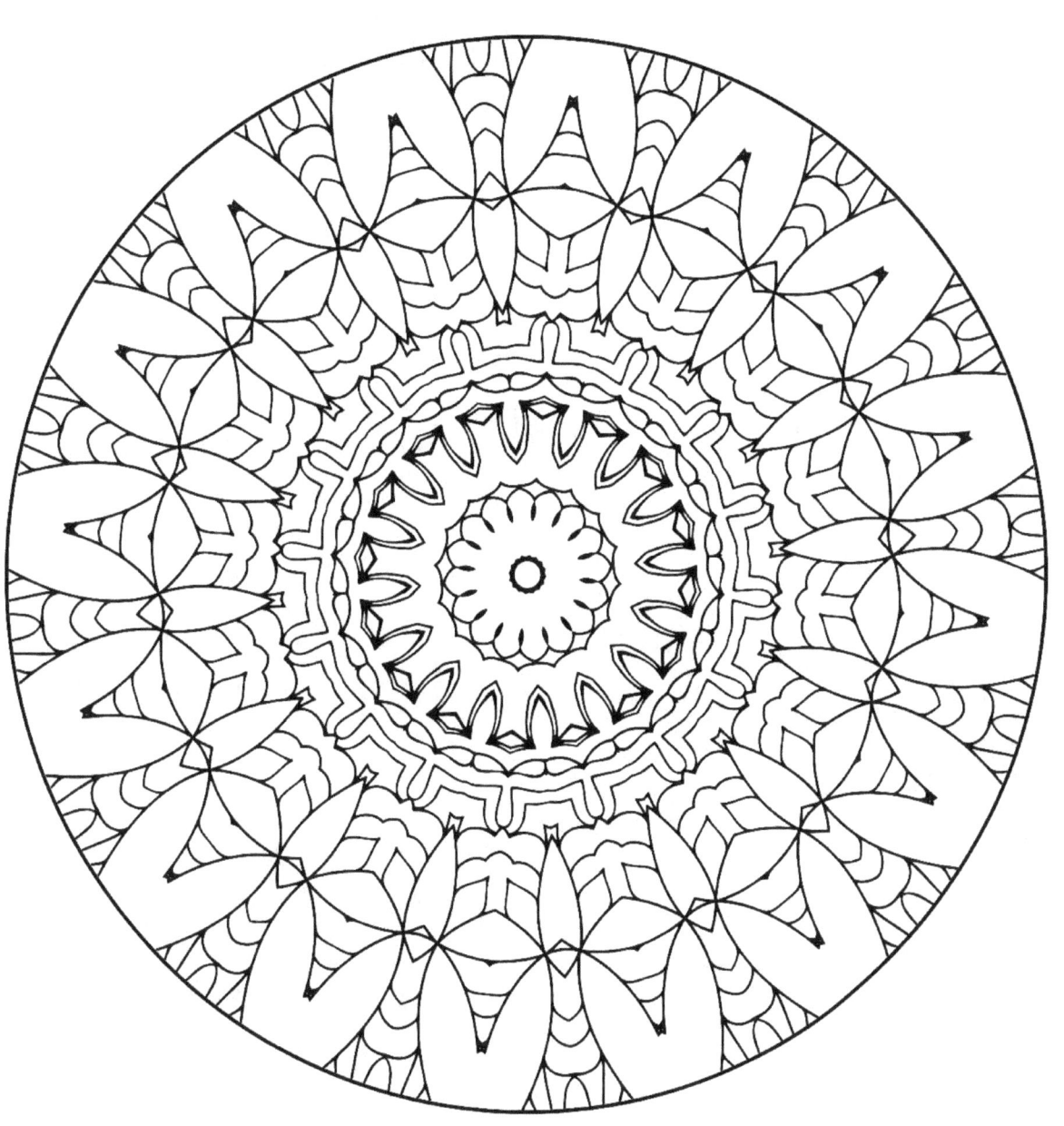

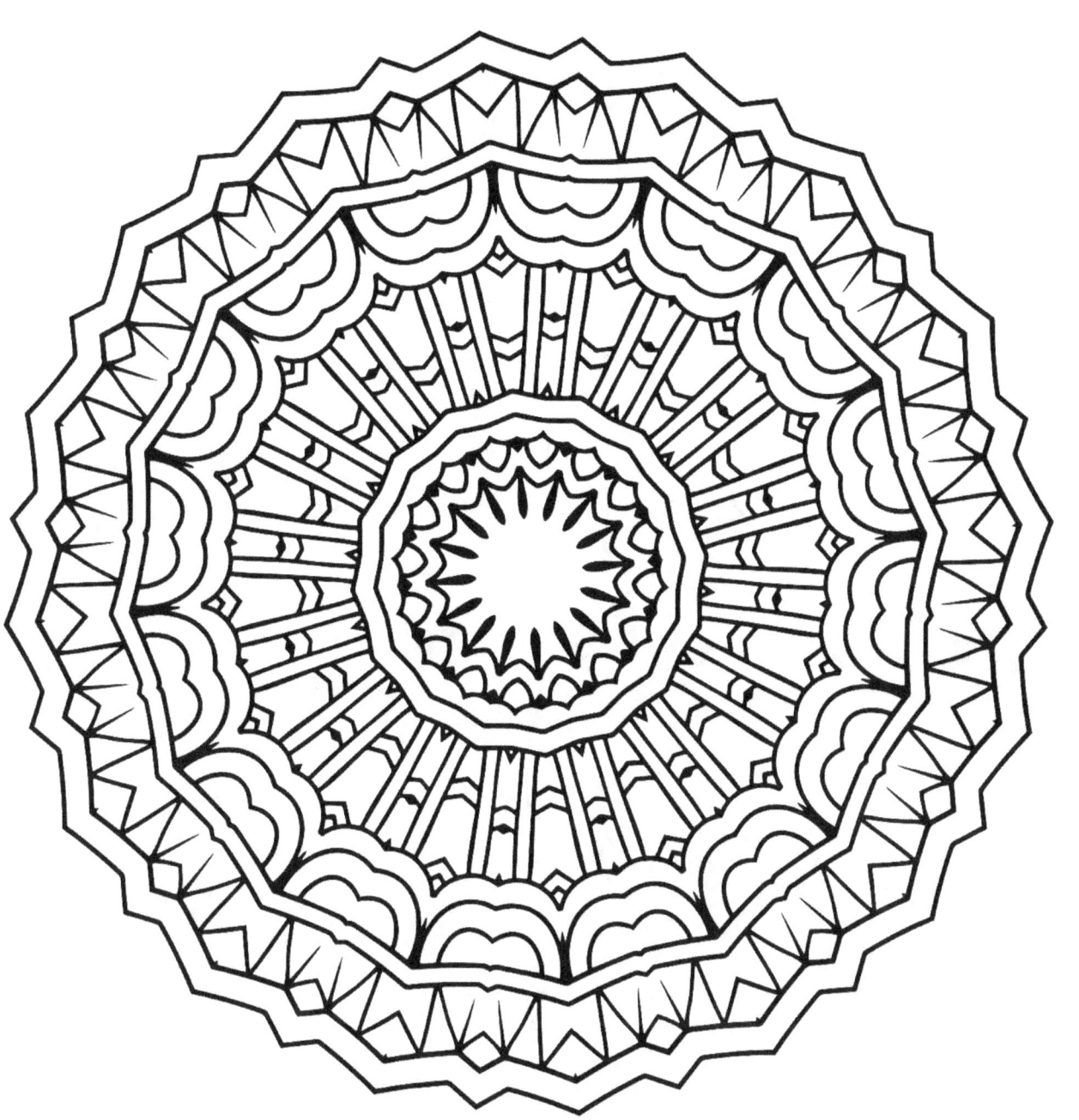

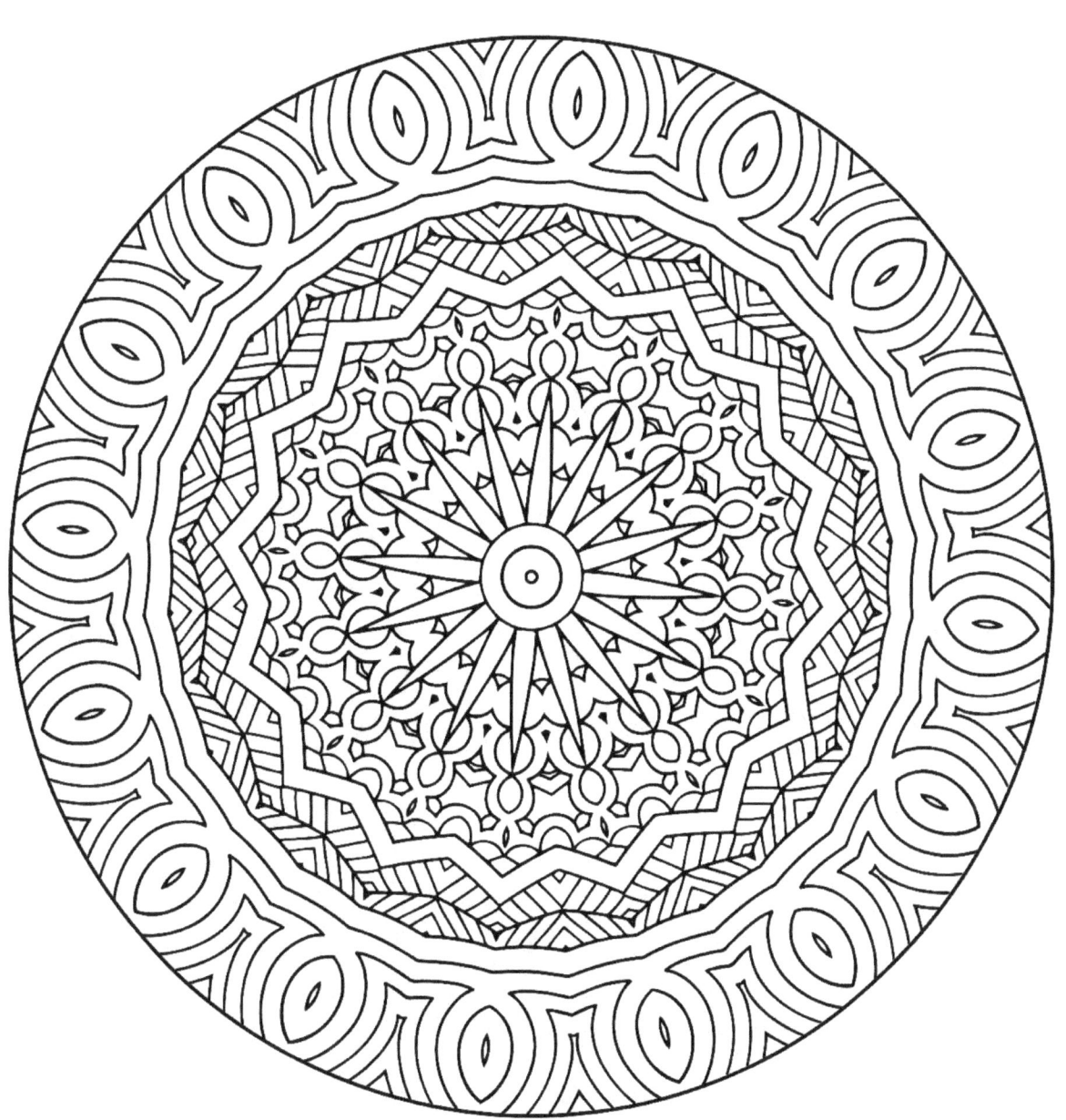

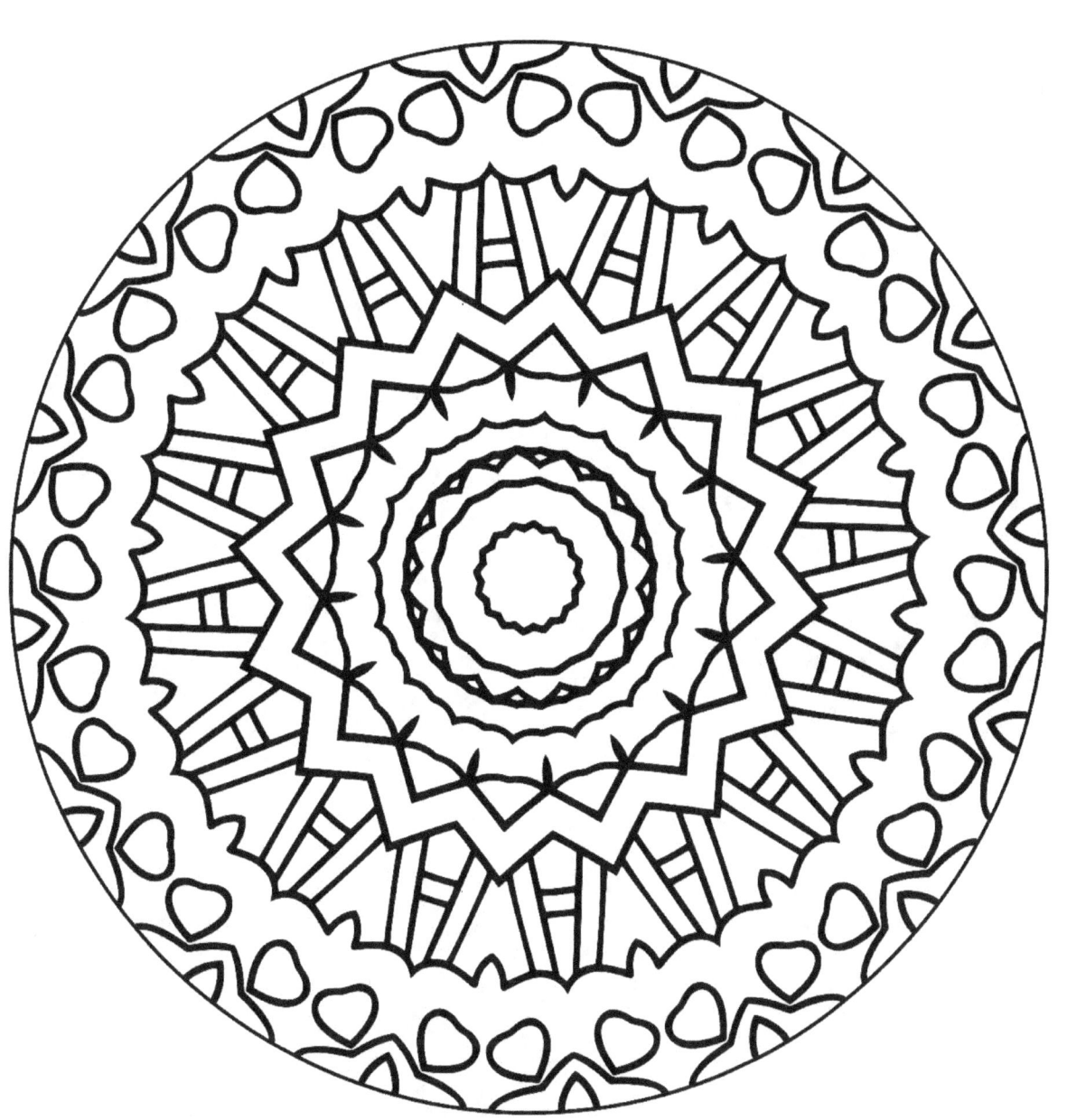

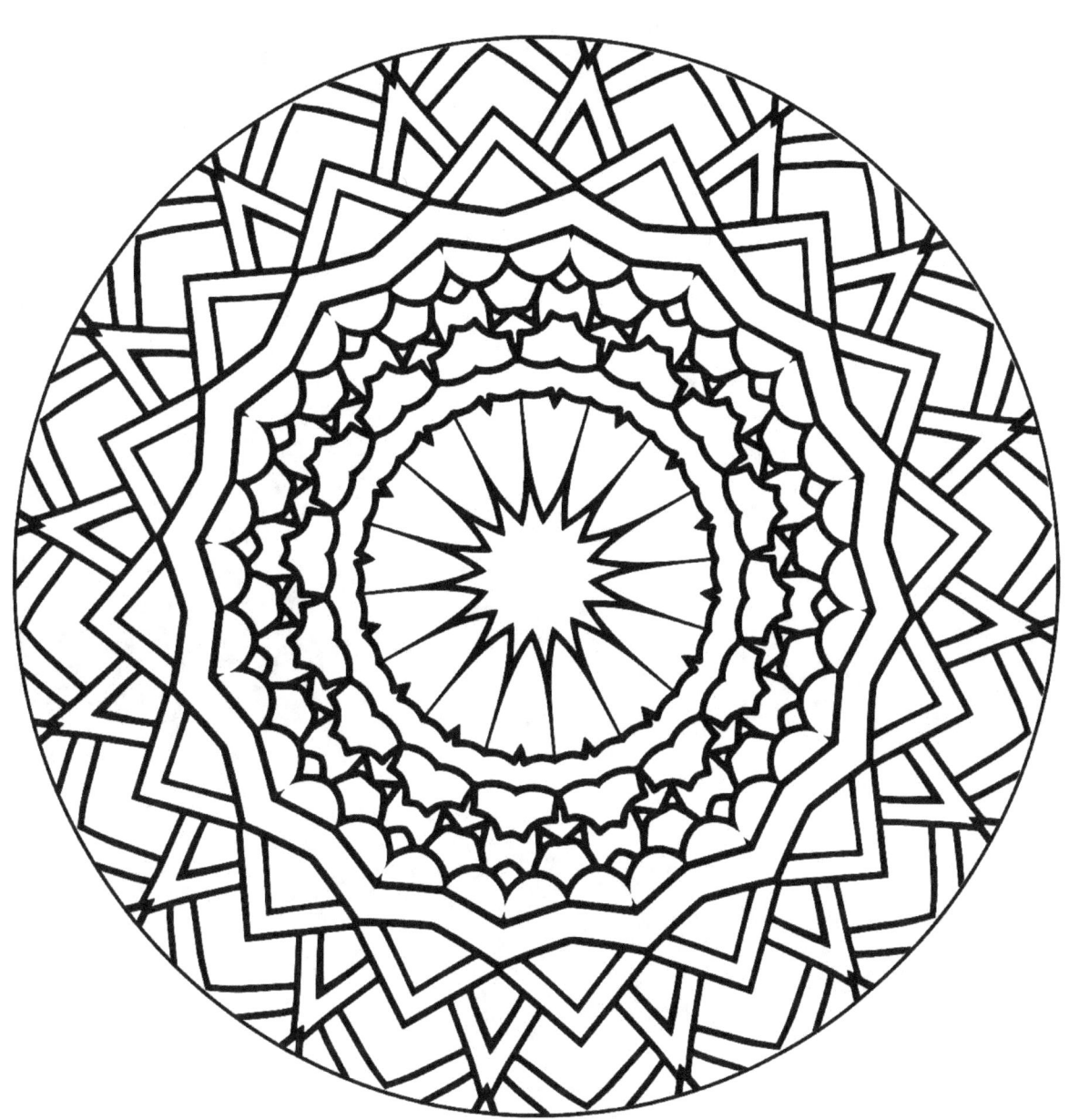

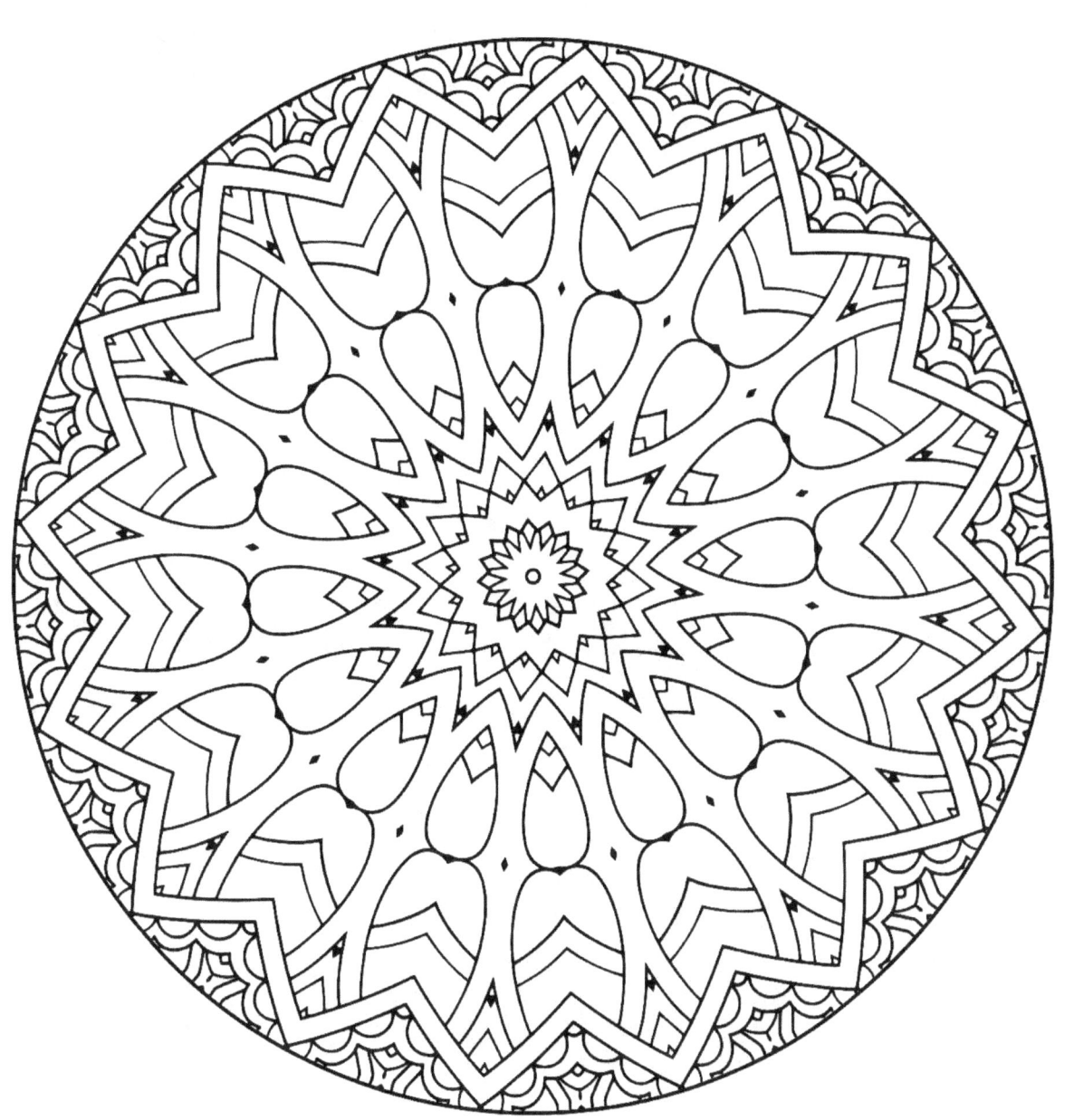

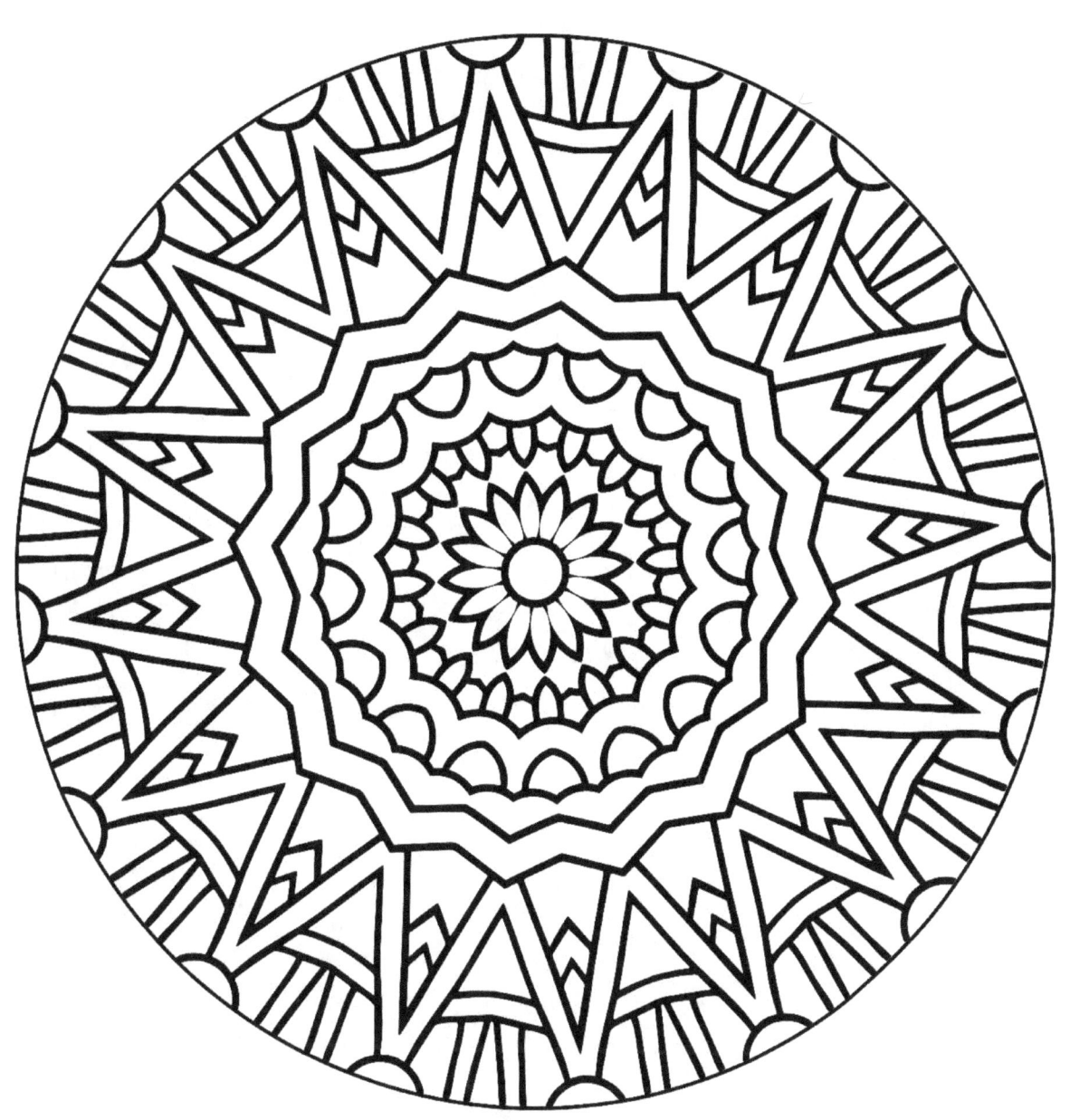

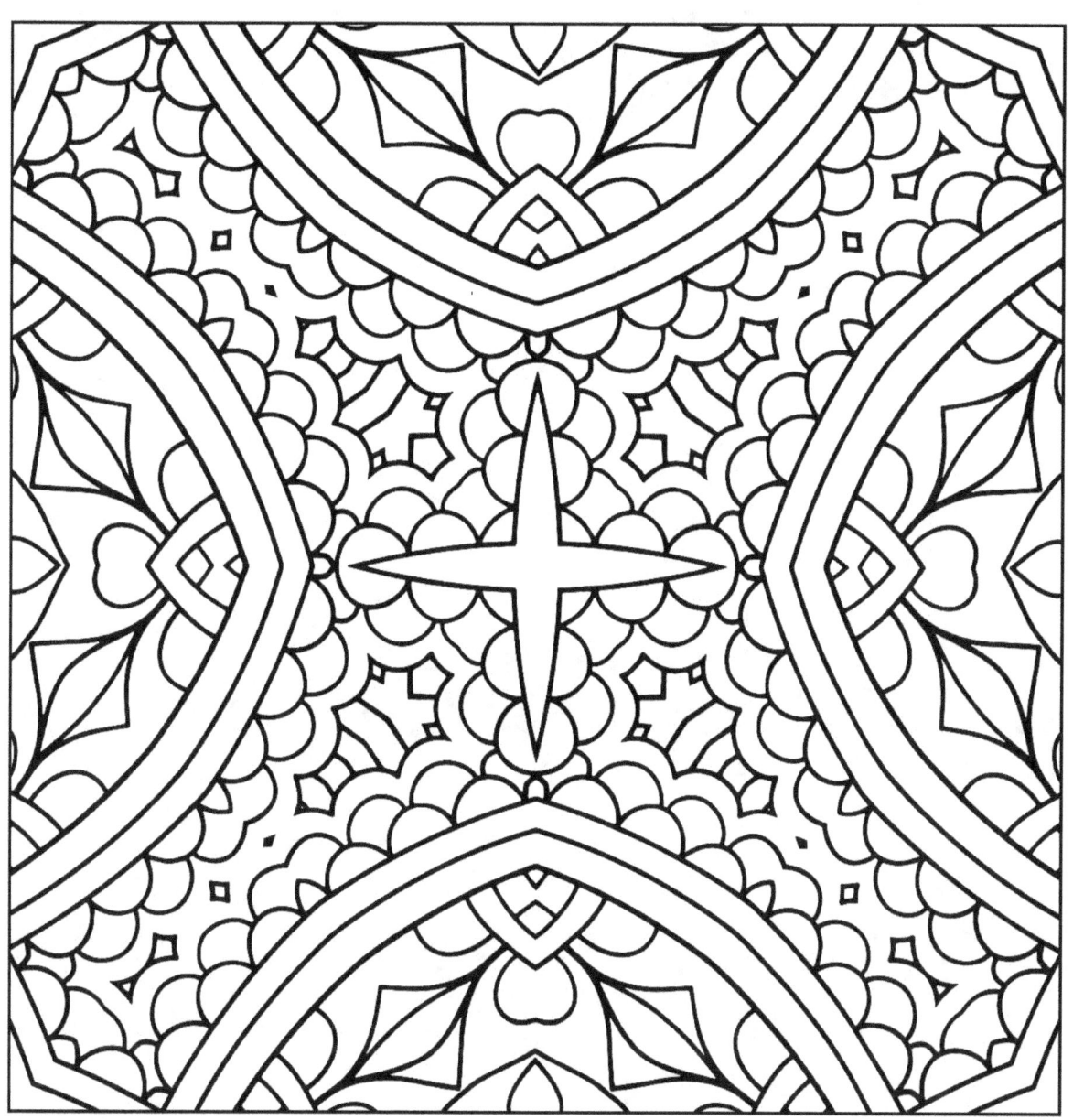

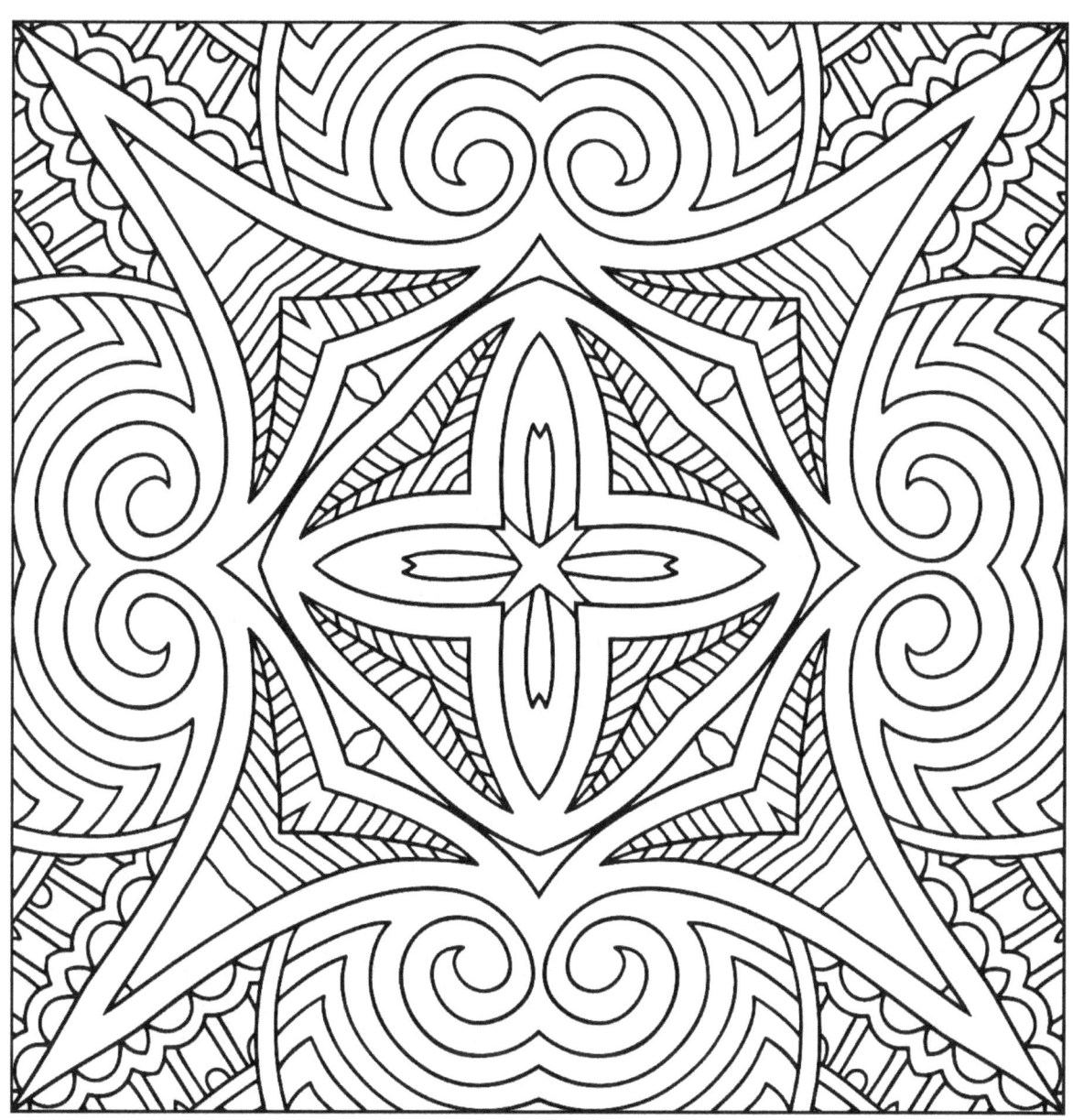

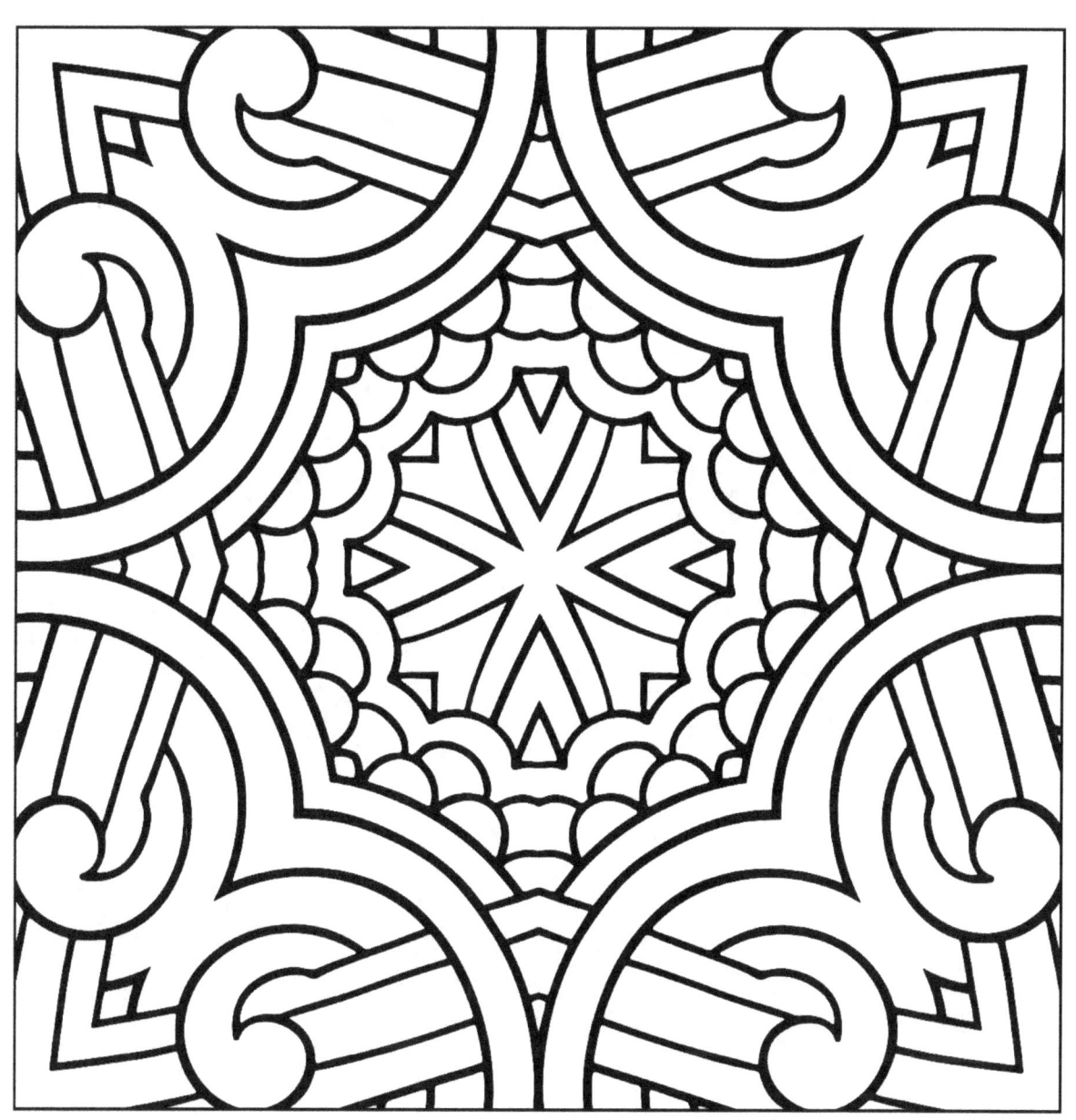

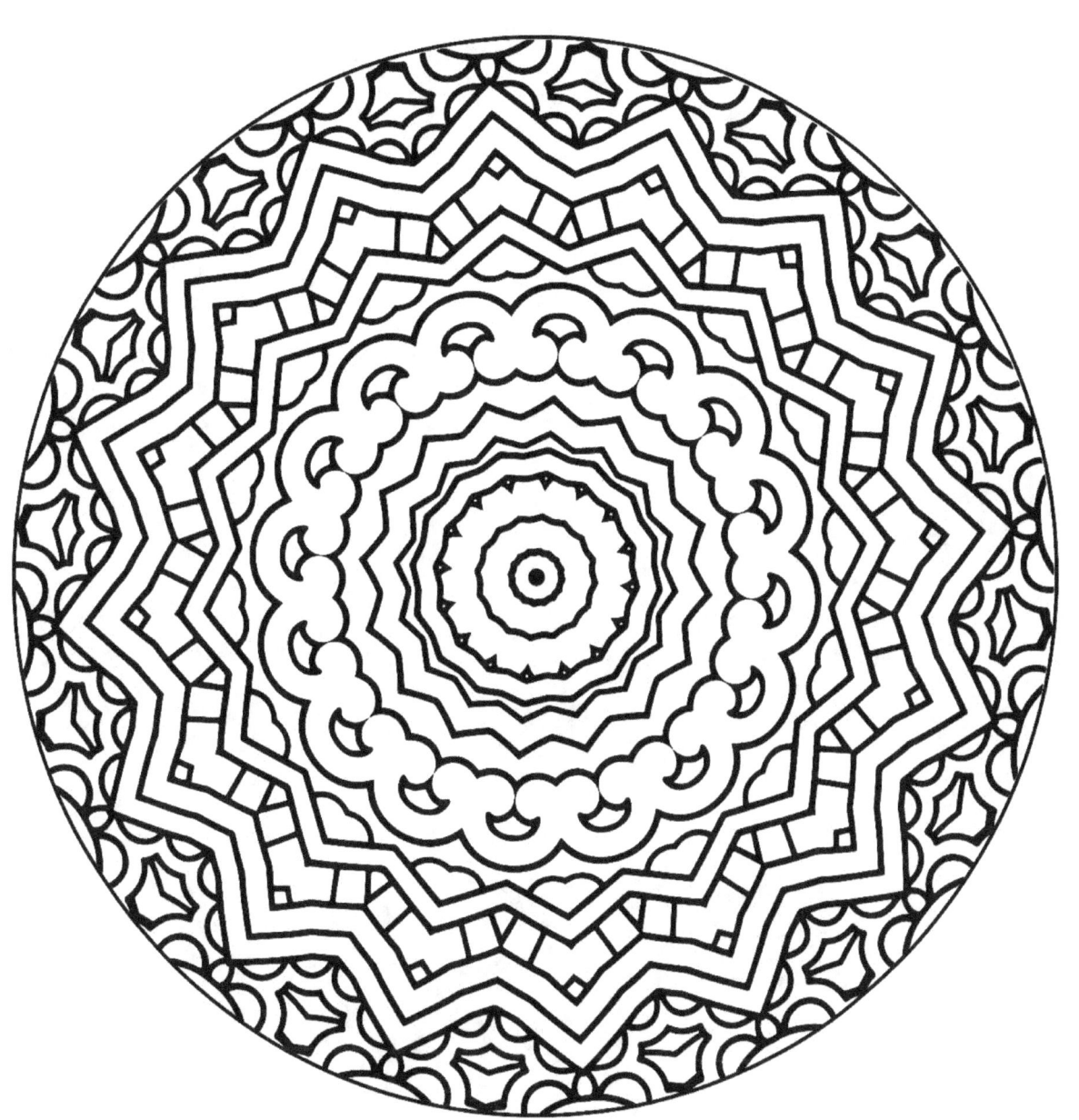

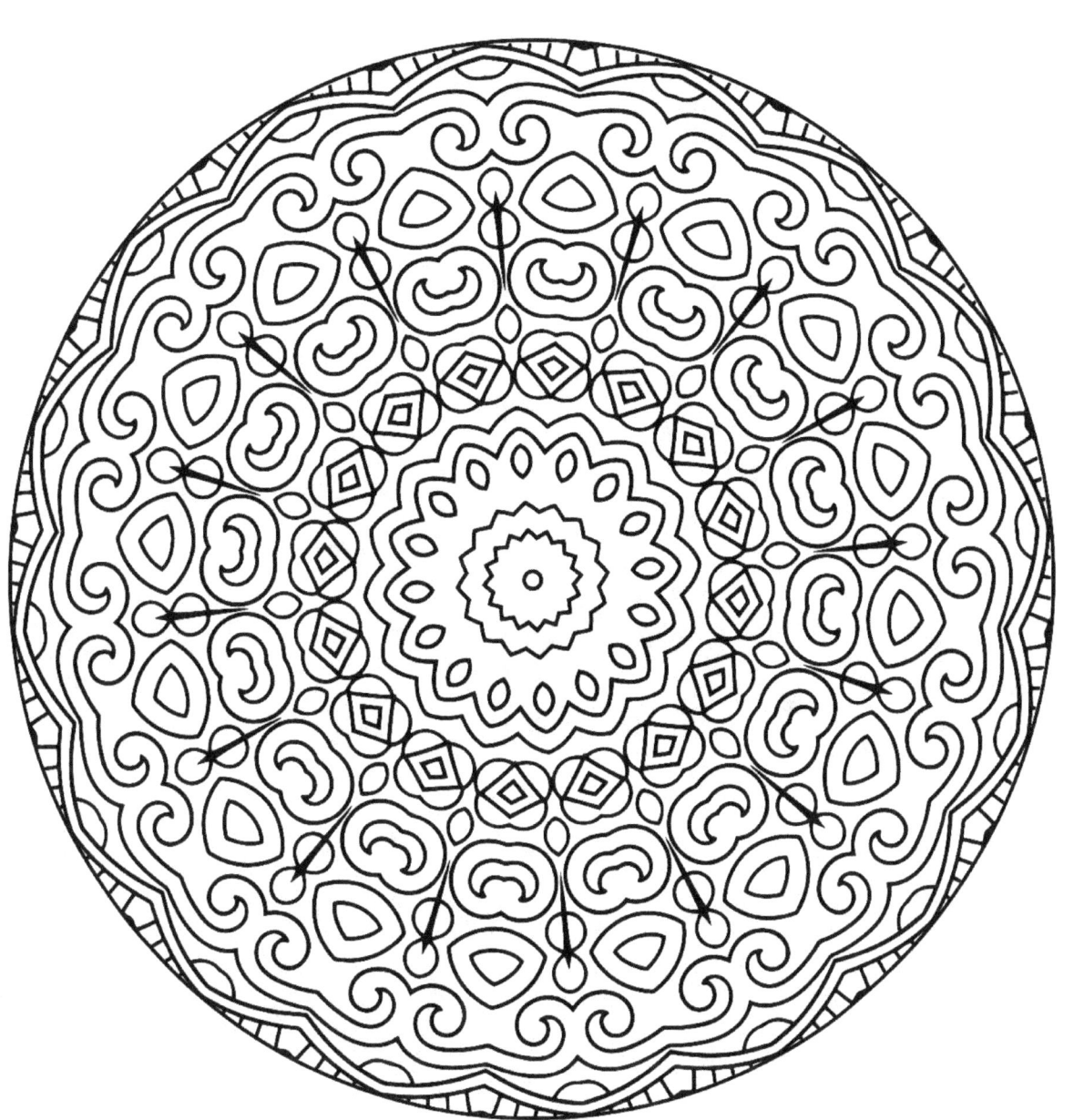

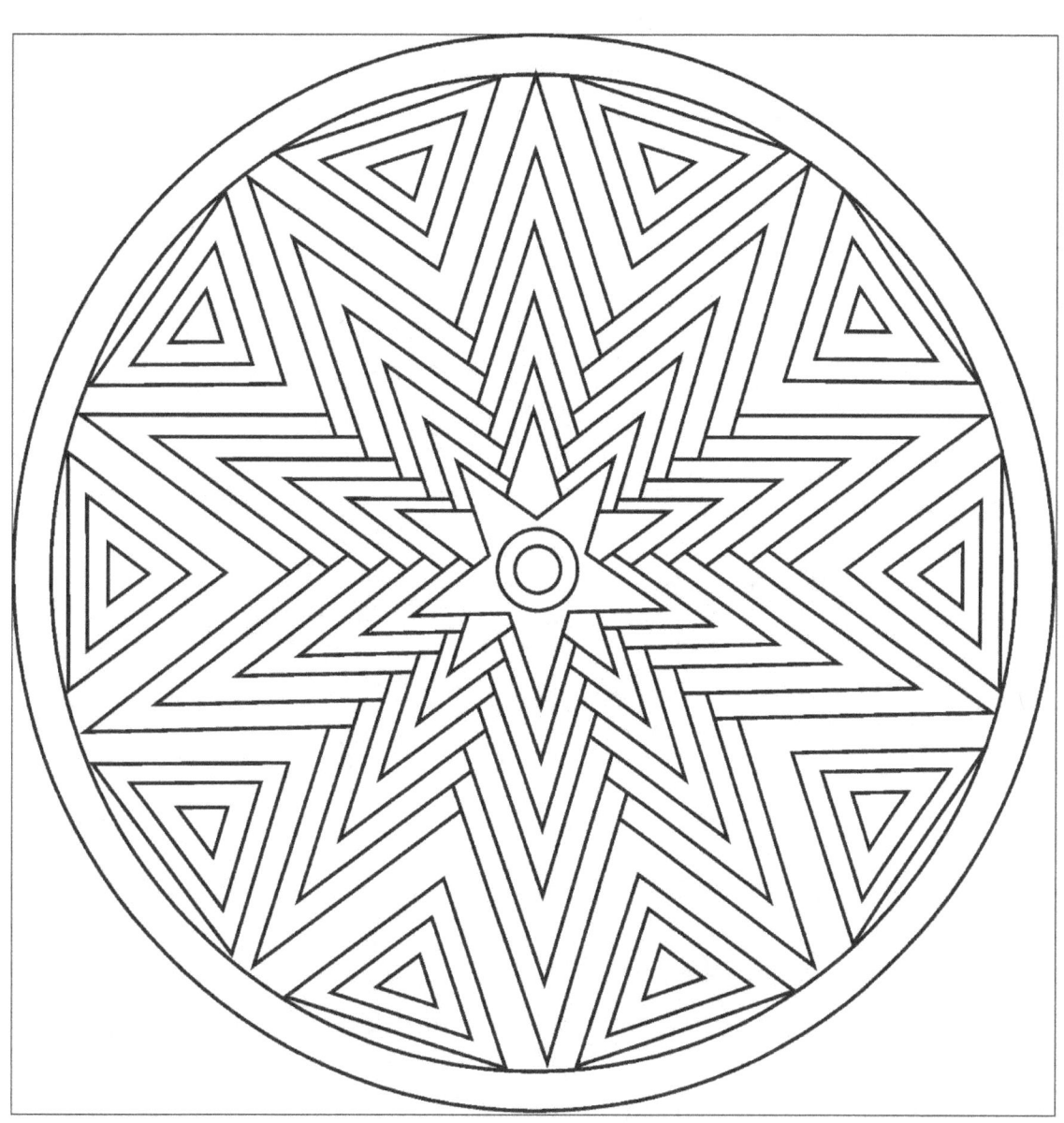

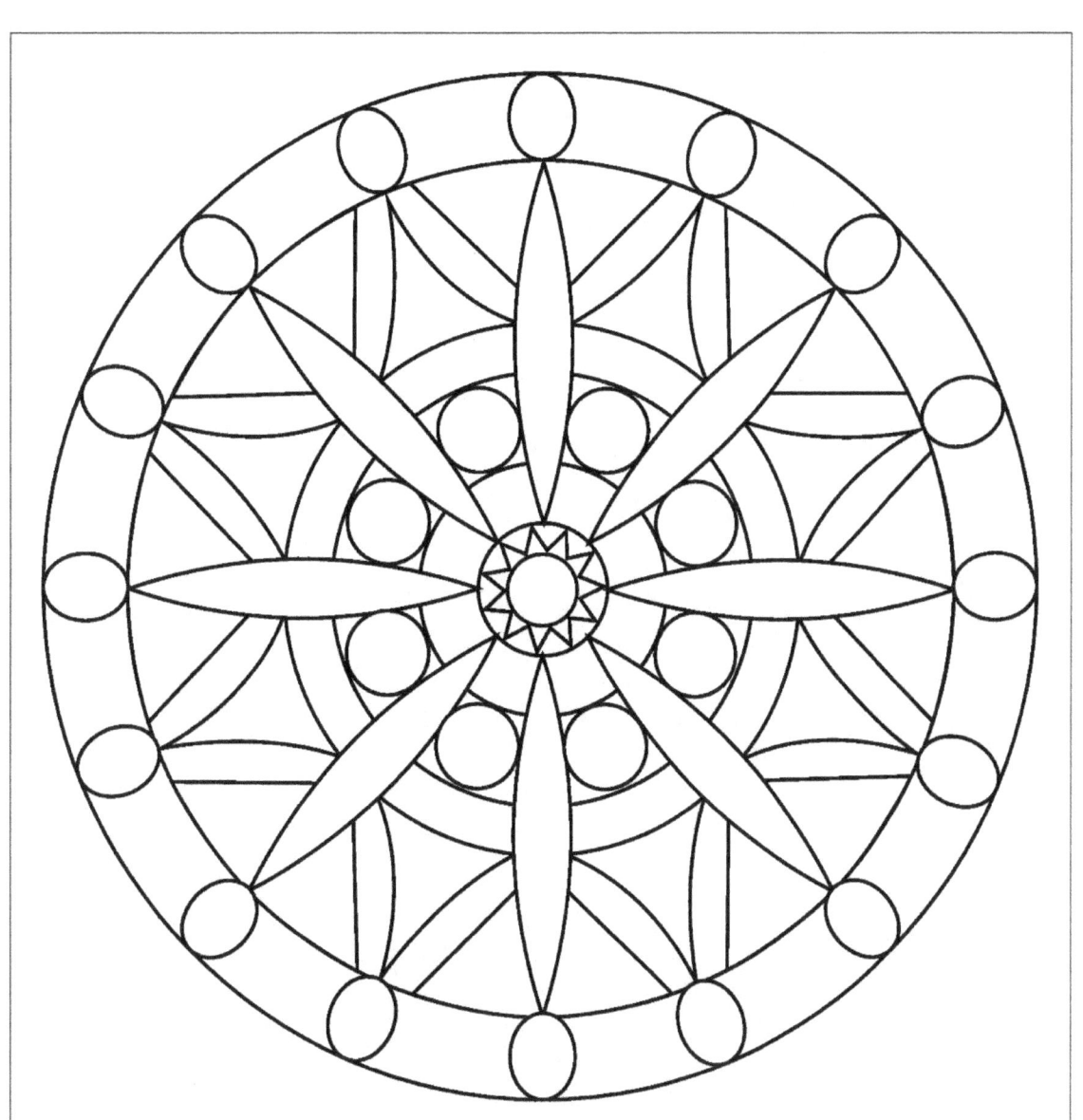

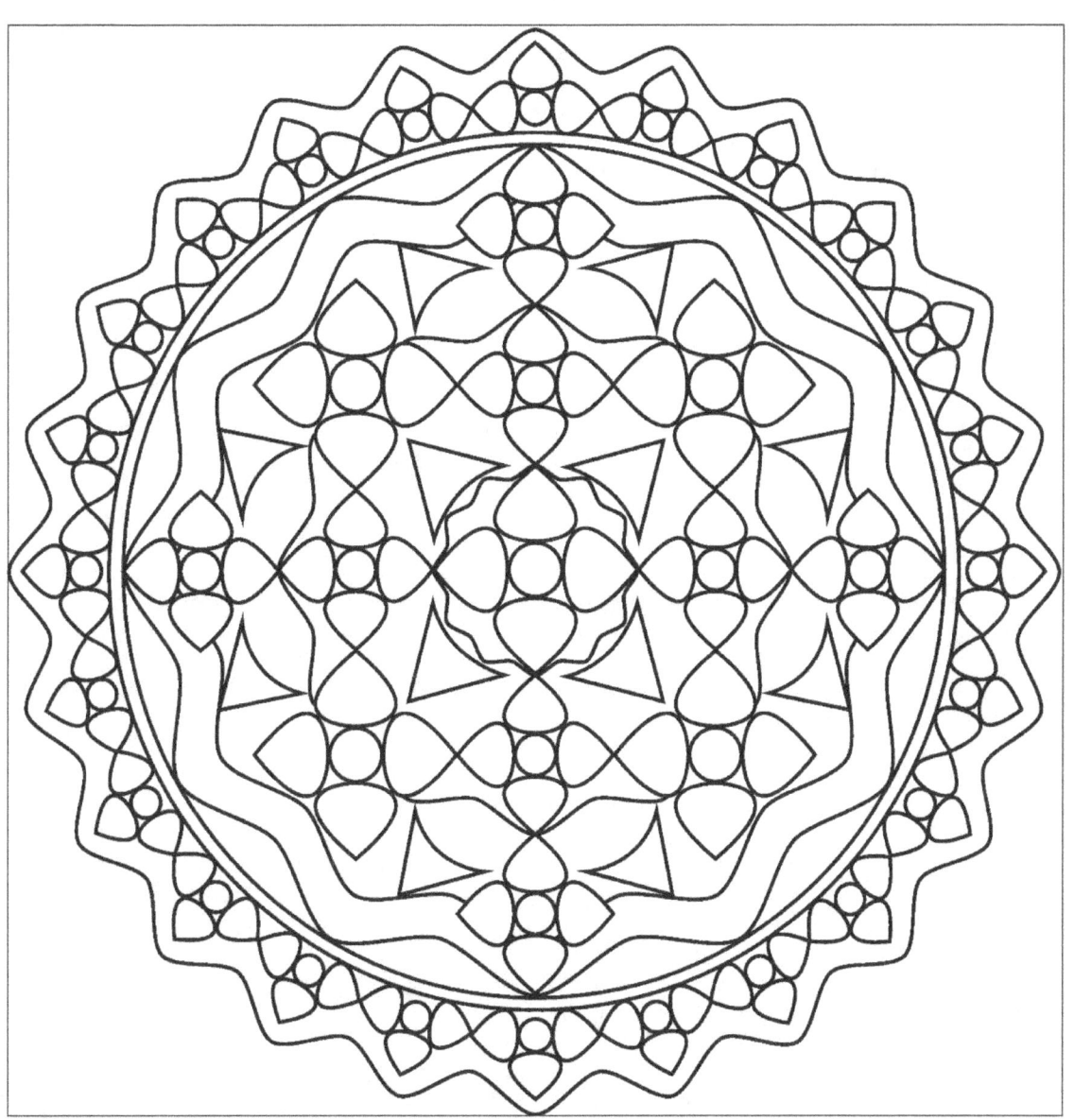

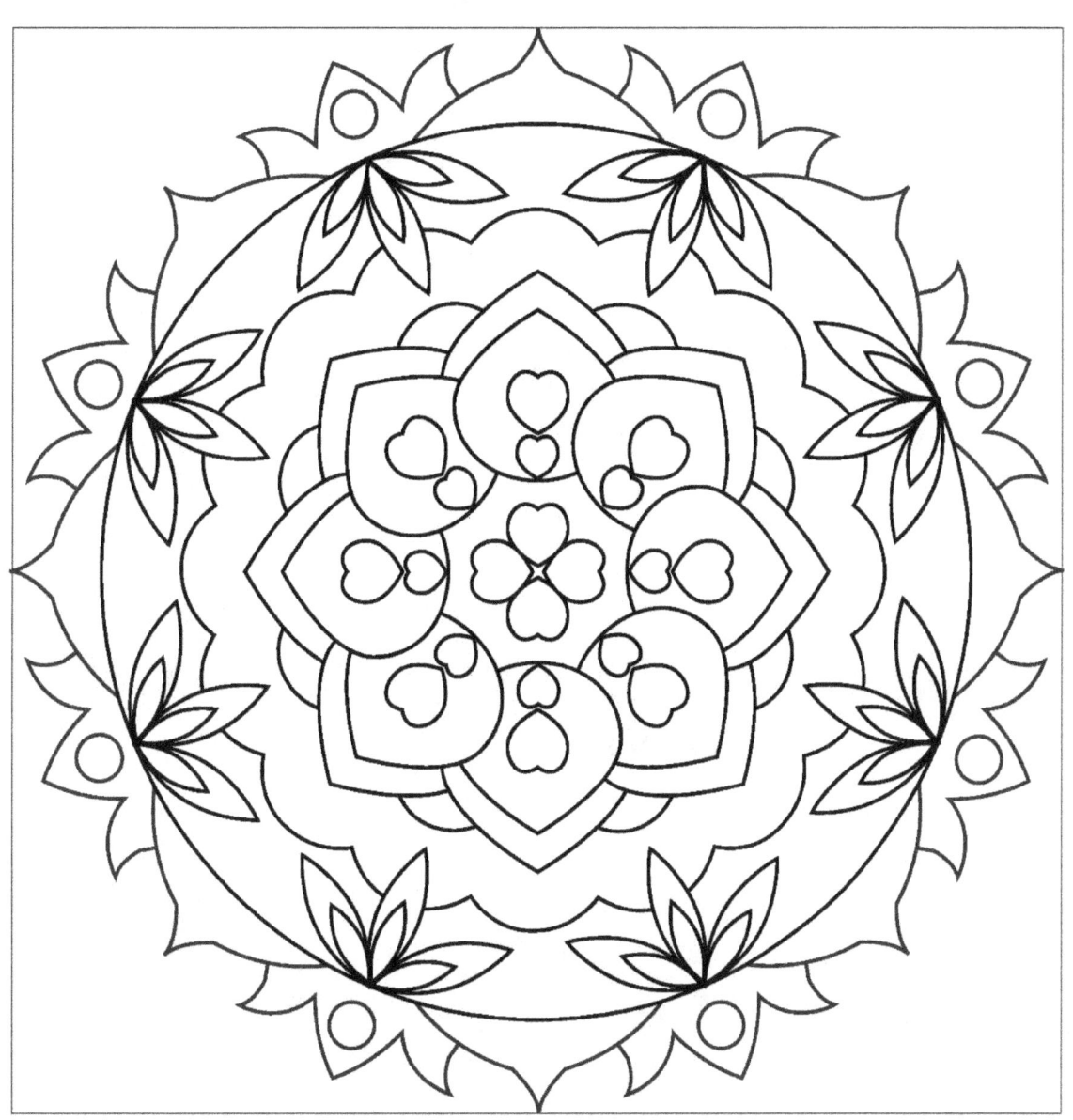

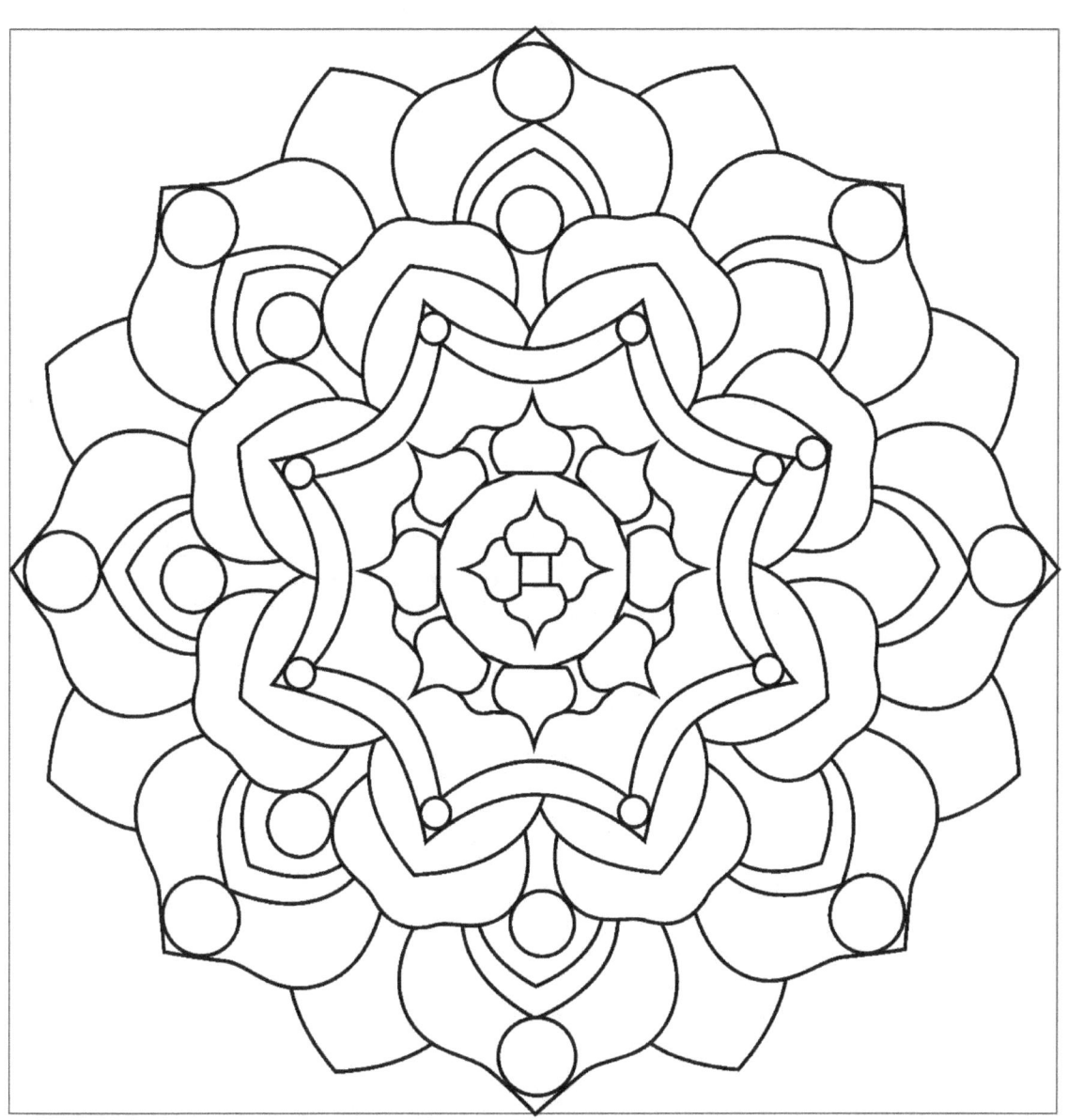

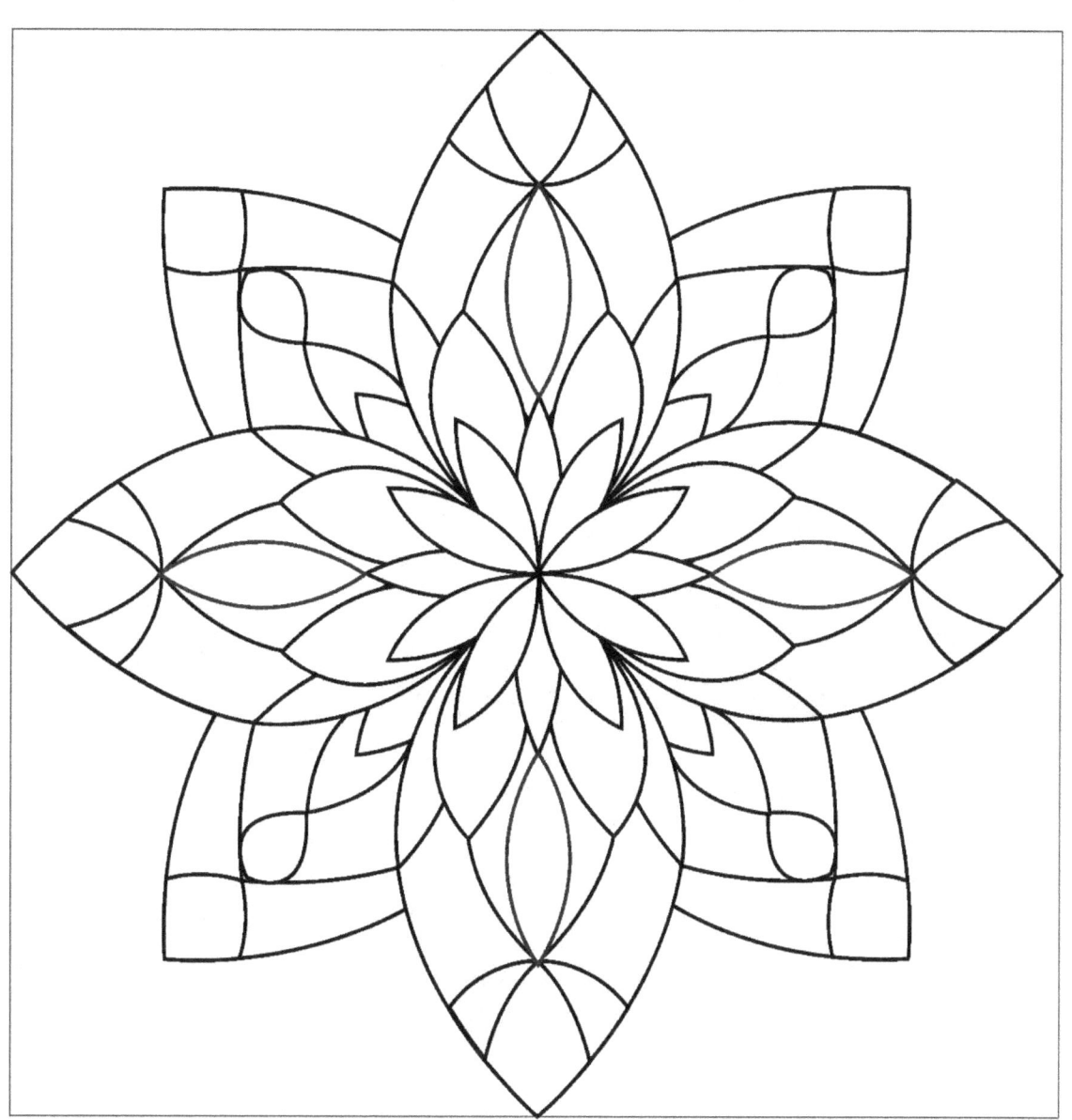

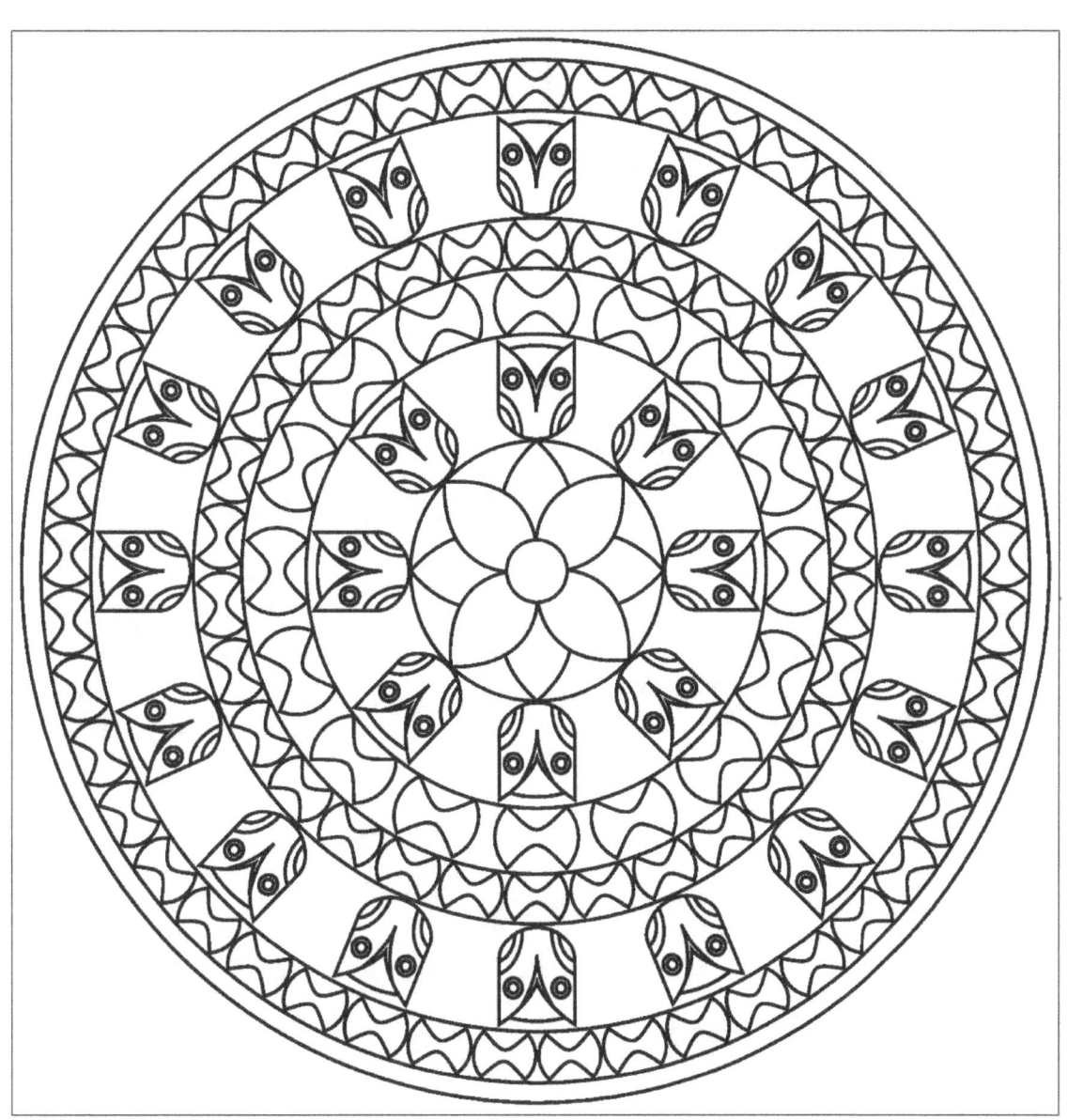

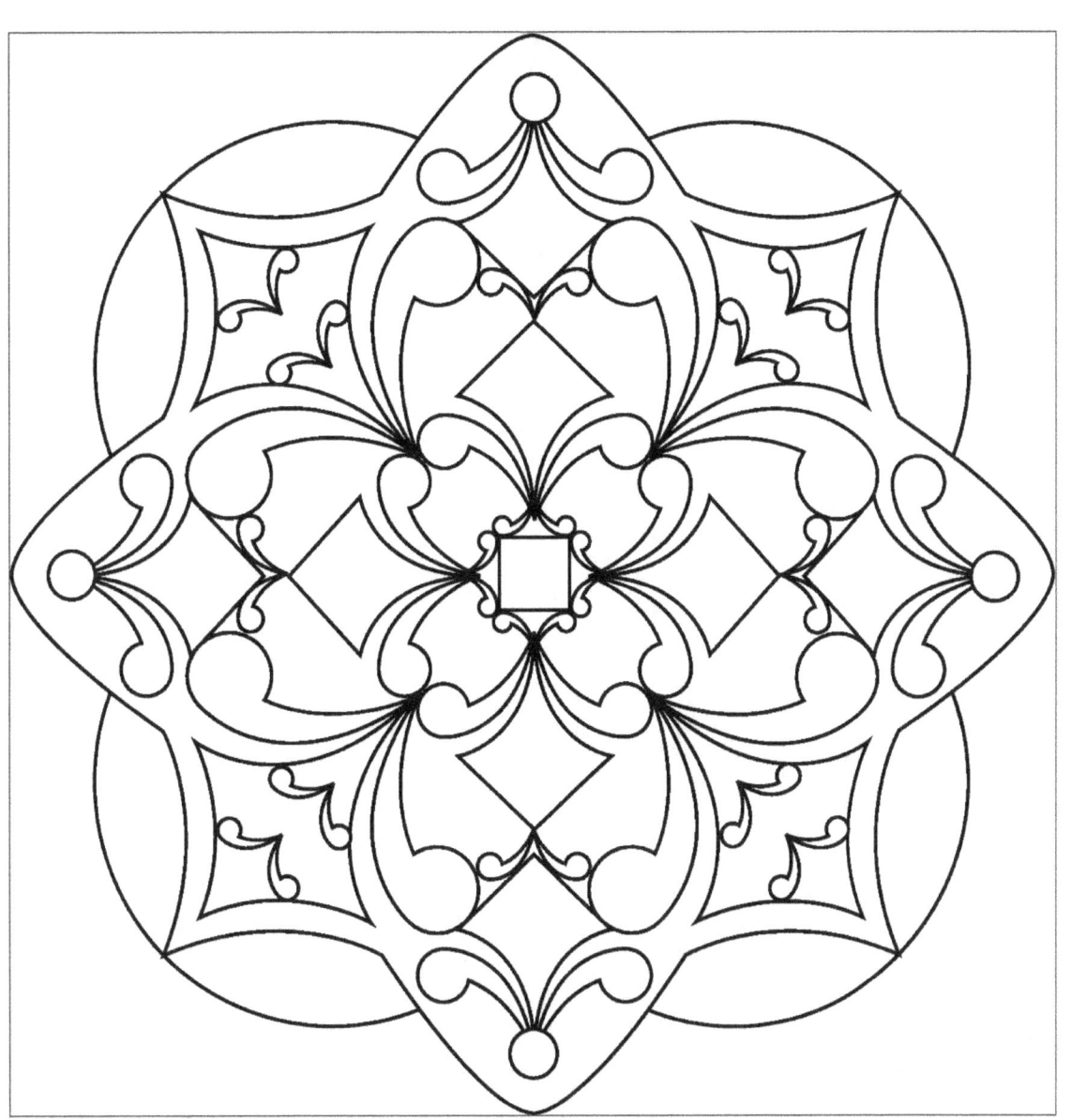

www.ingramcontent.com/pod-product-compliance
Lightning Source LLC
Chambersburg PA
CBHW081556170526
45166CB00009B/2714